FROM THE ROCK
TO THE GATES OF HELL

FROM THE ROCK
TO THE GATES OF HELL

by

Andrew W. Blackwood, Jr.

BAKER BOOK HOUSE
Grand Rapids, Michigan

FROM THE ROCK TO THE GATES OF HELL
Library of Congress Catalog Card Number: 68-19203
Copyright, 1968, by Baker Book House Company
Printed in the United States of America

To Nancy

Acknowledgments

Senator Abraham Ribicoff has graciously allowed me to quote from a speech given at the 40th Annual Meeting of the National Staff — Board of National Missions of the United Presbyterian Church of the United States of America on September 13th, 1966.

The following authors and publishers have kindly given permission to quote from copyright material:

Katallagate, Berea College Station, Berea, Kentucky.
"Events and Pseudo-Events," Thomas Merton, Summer Issue, 1966.

J. B. Lippincott Company, Philadelphia,
The Comfortable Pew, Pierre Berton, 1965.

The Macmillan Company, New York.
Letters and Papers from Prison, Dietrich Bonhoeffer, 1962.
Ethics, Dietrich Bonhoeffer, 1955.

New Christian, Prism Publications, London.
"The Coming Non-Church," June 2, 1966.

The National Observer, Silver Spring, Maryland.
"Religion and Metropolis," August 15, 1966.

Richard R. Smith, New York.
Under Orders, The Autobiography of William Lawrence Sullivan, 1944.

The Wall Street Journal, New York.
"Empty Pulpits," June 8, 1965.

The Westminster Press, Philadelphia, Pennsylvania.
The Gospel of Christian Atheism, Thomas J. J. Altizer, 1966.

The Bible text in this publication, unless otherwise indicated, is from the *Revised Standard Version of the Bible,* copyrighted 1946 and 1952, by the Division of Christian Education, National Council of Churches, and used by permission.

Contents

Foreword

In the following pages I advance the revolutionary thesis that our Savior probably knew what He was doing when He founded a Church on earth. Many contemporary theologians are in apparent disagreement; at least they write provocative articles about the future non-church. Most of what they say positively is well said; they advise us to do what we should have been doing all along. If we had been up to our ears in society's trouble, we wouldn't have so much trouble of our own today, and society might be a little less messy. I agree. I differ when theologians propose that we shelve the imperfect institution called the Church.

I believe that Christians need to assemble at fairly regular intervals (when physically possible) to do the sort of thing we are supposed to do at public worship. I believe that we need some kind of Church organization — perhaps about a tenth as much as we now have. I think that, by and large, it is a pretty good idea to have a few clergymen around who dedicate most of their working hours to the Church's work. I believe that Church buildings are valuable aids to Christian faith and life, which is not the same as defending the present duplication of buildings and staff, where a congregation expends most of its effort maintaining a mausoleum. I believe that the on-going congregation is important, though not all-important. A congregation means a group of people who live or work in such proximity that they can meet more or less regularly to pray and think and plan. The Church is universal, but the members aren't. We need some kind of home base to touch occasionally.

I believe that the Lord's long-term response to human need is the Church; not the Church invisible but the visible and frequently irritating organization. I know how feeble has been our response to the cry of pain, how many mistakes we have made, how often we have failed to act. I propose that we correct our faults and get on with the job. I doubt that we could make a significant contribution by going out of business.

I believe that the Church is at once a divine society and a human organization, which means we must look at the Church through spectacles containing two very different lenses — theology and sociology — if we hope to examine the reality. I know the painful wrench of turning from a theological study of the Church — say in Ephesians — to the problems of plumbing or a squabble in the choir. The pain is necessary if we are to think about the Church.

Although I am no sociologist, I examine here the sort of thing a social scientist examines: a human organization, with many defects and some virtues. I claim to be a theologian only to the degree that every Christian must try to think logically about God. In my capacity as theologian (junior grade) I look at the self-same organization and find something invisible to the social scientist: occasional sparks of eternal, divine light.

I want to thank many persons who have helped me in reaching my revolutionary conclusions, though I hasten to exculpate them from responsibility for my reactions to their thoughts. What follows is in no sense a bibliography about the Church; from the dozens of excellent books I have studied I have chosen for mention a few that bristle with interesting ideas.

My thoughts about the Church, and almost everything else, have been strongly influenced by John Calvin, whose doctrine of the Church was forged by the clash between transcendence and incarnation, which brings him near to the conflict I have mentioned between theology and sociology. Calvin sees the Church, not as a divine society that somehow has been misplaced, and not as a human society filled with bumbling good intentions, but as a miracle of grace operating on earth. His primary concern is with the visible Church, our mother: "We are conceived by her, born of her, nourished at her breast, and continually preserved under her care and government till we are divested of this mortal flesh, and 'become like angels.'" (*Institutes* IV.I.4). The visible Church is my primary concern.

The comments in Chapter 7 about the worker-priest movement are based upon Gregor Siefer's thesis, *The Church and
Industrial Society*. The author is a Roman Catholic priest
whose love for his Church leads him to criticize her leaders
bitterly when he thinks they have been wrong. His prose
is anything but exciting; he loses the reader in a jungle of
footnotes; sometimes you must hack your way through with
a machete to learn what is being said. But I have found myself a better Protestant because I have examined my faith
from an unaccustomed angle, through the eyes of a great-
hearted, cool-headed Roman Catholic priest, who recognizes
the important differences between the methods and the principles of sociology and theology, and wisely concludes that
the nature of his subject requires him to risk the danger of
falling between two stools.

I express my gratitude to Dietrich Bonhoeffer in Chapter 8,
especially for his work *Sanctorum Communio*, which he calls
A Dogmatic Inquiry into the Sociology of the Church. He
raises some of the questions that Siefer raises about the
difficulty of welding dissimilar metals, and comes to much
the same conclusion.

George Macleod's brief pamphlet, *We Shall Rebuild*, more
than any other book from the twentieth century, has influenced my thinking about the Church. This started out to
explain the Iona Community; but, since George Macleod is
the man God made him, the pamphlet gets to the heart
of the matter: What is the Church all about? Dr. Macleod is
never reluctant to discuss weakness and stupidity within the
Church or anywhere else. Scotland is full of sore toes he has
trampled. Every time I reread his book my own get a little
more tender. But, sore toes and all, I have tried to the best
of my ability to express here some of the big ideas in *We Shall
Rebuild*.

Once in a review I saw mentioned *The Deployment and
Payment of the Clergy*, by Leslie Paul, a sociologist whom the
Church of England commissioned to examine the matters
mentioned in the title. I ordered a copy expecting to find
about 10 per cent applicable to the American scene, where
we stand to benefit from good ideas, no matter where they
come from.

To my surprise I found that about 90 per cent of the Paul Report applies to us in the United States. England has pretty much the same kind of problems we have: growing cities and dwindling rural population, Church buildings located where the people aren't, institutions kept going because grandma went there while the bulk of society has no shadow of interest in the gospel or the Church. The chief difference is that the Church in (and of) England knows she is in trouble, but our fiscal prosperity has blinded us to our poverty. Our predecessors in Laodicea had the same difficulty and the good Lord didn't give up; I dare say He will get us straightened out finally. I found the Paul Report of great value, simply because it deals with the earthy, commercial questions which the theologian can ignore but which the Church must answer if the divine society is to function.

When I was about twelve years old I read an article, brilliantly entitled, "What's Wrong with the Church?" I think it was in the *Saturday Evening Post*. I've been reading it about once a month ever since, in newspapers, magazines, pamphlets, and books. After my first reading I decided that the Church in the United States couldn't possibly survive until I had reached voting age. By now I have become more cautious about predicting the Church's death. People have been prematurely conducting her funeral service for two thousand years.

The best presentation of what's-wrong-with-the-Church I can remember is that by Pierre Berton, *The Comfortable Pew*, mentioned in Chapter 8. By long odds the funniest presentation is *How to Become a Bishop without Being Religious*, by Charles Merrill Smith. Sometimes the humor verges on blasphemy, but it's nowhere near so blasphemous as the pious perversions of the gospel that Smith is discussing.

Sometimes the article "What's-wrong-with-the-Church" disgusts me by its superficiality, sometimes it annoys me, and sometimes it makes me think. To all of our critics whose work falls in the last mentioned category, I express my thanks.

For contemporary news articles about the Church I find more depth (if less breadth) in *The National Observer* and sometimes in *The Wall Street Journal* than in most of the religious press. These journals present the facts without the hysteria that some news magazines provide, and without pleading a cause as the religious press frequently does. Some comments in Chapter 7 are based upon "Religion and Metropolis," a news story in *The National Observer,* issue of August 15, 1966, about the Metropolitan Associates of Philadelphia. I know nothing concerning the group beyond the news story; so I am in no position to endorse or to condemn. The goals of the group, as reported in the story, seem to me the contemporary expression of many goals that Jesus set. The quotation from *The Wall Street Journal* in Chapter 2 is taken from a sobering news story, "Empty Pulpits," in the issue of June 8, 1965.

Several individuals have helped me greatly. First, and always most important, Mrs. Blackwood who, among other things, sat with an expectant look on her lovely face while listening to one of the following sermons for the thirteenth time. She even laughed at the right place. My co-workers and valued friends — the Reverend Robert Battles, the Reverend John Thomas Holmes, and the Reverend Martin Griffith — have read the manuscript and made valuable criticism. They have helped, far more than they will ever know, in thousands of informal discussions about the Church and everything else, and chiefly by living the faith they proclaim. Professor Norvin Hein of Yale Seminary knows the answers to more questions than any other man in the United States. He has given generously of time and information about obscure details. Mrs. Homer Vivian has demonstrated unending patience with my abominable writing and has gone far beyond the call of duty in preparing the manuscript.

Mostly I want to thank the congregations with whom I have served, particularly that in West Palm Beach, Florida, where my ideas about the Church were hammered into shape. The book that follows is presented as a series of sermons. The congregation is patient and long-suffering, though not quite so patient as the book might suggest in its present form. Several chapters would take about an hour and three-quarters for me to deliver, and I'm afraid the roast might start burning before I was through. Even so, all the material here has been preached to real live people whom I love. This fact accounts for several ommissions that will grieve theolo-

gians (senior grade). Nowhere do I raise such questions as
the relationship between the Church and the Kingdom. Theologians can give, and have given, every possible answer to
the question. But I don't remember that anyone has ever
asked me. In preaching I try to answer the questions that
people ask me on Tuesday and Wednesday.

People who love the Church, the visible and sometimes
exasperating institution, have asked every question that I
have attempted here to answer. I know why Jacob referred
to his encounter with the Holy Spirit as wrestling; I have
struggled with theologians, sociologists, critics, friends, occasional enemies, and with the Holy Spirit in arriving at the
answers given.

1

WHEN THE CHURCH WAS BORN
Matthew 16:13-19

Matthew 16:13-19

Now when Jesus came into the district of Caesarea Philippi, he asked his disciples, "Who do men say that the Son of man is?" And they said, "Some say John the Baptist, others say Elijah, and others Jeremiah or one of the prophets." He said to them, "But who do you say that I am?" Simon Peter replied, "You are the Christ, the Son of the living God."

And Jesus answered him, "Blessed are you, Simon BarJona! For flesh and blood has not revealed this to you, but my Father who is in heaven. And I tell you, you are Peter, and on this rock I will build my church, and the gates of hell[1] shall not prevail against it. I will give you the keys of the kingdom of heaven, and whatever you bind on earth shall be bound in heaven, and whatever you loose on earth shall be loosed in heaven."

---

[1] Authorized Version.

1

WHEN THE CHURCH WAS BORN

Matthew 16:13-19

Critics are asking if the Church can, or should, survive into the twenty-first century. Recently I read an article, "The Coming Non-Church," where the author gloomily surveys the ecclesiastical edifice and announces, "We can tinker with it here and there, but in the end there is only one course of action possible: like a building with dry rot through most of its woodwork, you must tear out the lot and start again." The writer is a Christian, not an enemy of Christ, who sees the institutional Church as the chief obstacle to the practice of Christ-like love in modern society.

Those who would destroy the present institution have adopted the slogan "religionless Christianity" as the guideline for our future development. The forms of religion through which Christians expressed their faith have been changing for nineteen centuries. I pray for many and radical changes in the immediate future. I strongly suspect, however, that when the changes have been made there will remain on earth a visible institution called the Church. Jesus thought it would stay here long enough to batter in the gates of hell, which look quite formidable as the twentieth century enters its last third.

THE EASY QUESTION AND THE HARD ONE

At Caesarea Philippi Jesus asked two questions; the answer to the second brought the Church into being. The first ques-

19

tion is easy. "Who do men say that the Son of Man is?" To answer this today you need only patience and thoroughness. You can read what the Methodists, Baptists, Episcopalians, Mennonites, Roman Catholics, Unitarians, Jews, Mohammedans, and atheists say about Jesus Christ. If you do your homework carefully, you can then give a thoughtful, reasoned reply to the question. If you do it carefully enough, you will likewise discover that people sometimes say one thing with their lips and another with their lives. Pointing out the discrepancy between Christian faith and practice has long been a popular amusement. Answering the second question detracts from the amusement, though. It leaves you wondering about the discrepancy between your own faith and your own practice.

The easy question led to the hard one. "But who do you say that I am?" The bewildering abundance of contradictory answers shows that the question is important. Sincere people have been asking it for twenty centuries. We simply do not ask this about other great historical figures from the Hellenistic age. Who do you say was Alexander the Great? Who do you say was Julius Caesar? Who do you say was Cicero or Ovid? It sounds silly. You don't need to make a decision about any of these men. If you can't answer from memory, you can look it up. Who do you say is Jesus? The encyclopedia can give valuable information, but the answer you live with is found by searching your heart, not in a reference book.

THE CHRISTIAN ANSWER

Simon Peter, the bluff, impulsive, always changeable Simon Peter, gave the Christian answer to the hard question. "You are the Christ, the Son of the living God."

The almost infinite variety of answers to the hard question can readily be separated into two groups. Some answer with Peter, that Christ is divine; others say that Jesus was a great Man.

Almost everyone agrees that Jesus, a Galilean Carpenter, became a traveling Rabbi and Physician, whose teaching has never been approached before or since for sublimity and penetration, and who was unjustly put to death by a Roman procurator. Call these the encyclopedia facts. Once in a while someone attempts to deny them, claiming that the historical Jesus is a myth, like Santa Claus or Paul Bunyan. But the world's serious scholars, Christian and non-Christian alike, have examined this recurring argument and asked, in effect, "How stupid can you get?" Almost everyone accepts the rough historical outline of Jesus' career, and then comes the division. Some say, "That's it. He was a great Man who was unjustly crucified." And others of us join with Simon Peter, saying, "You are the Christ, the Son of the living God."

Today we associate the name Jesus with the title Christ so readily that we interchange them without thought. Once I asked a young theologian — aged nine — what was Jesus' last name. He looked at me with a pitying look that comes so readily to the pre-adolescent face, and told me, "The Name is Jesus Christ, C-H-R-I-S-T." Last names are a relatively modern invention. In Nazareth, where there may have been a dozen boys with the name, he was called Jesus the son of Joseph. In Galilee and Jerusalem, he was called Jesus of Nazareth. His early disciples, and then the infant Church, learned to call Jesus by the title Christ.

The Greek word "Christ" means "the Anointed"; the Hebrew is "Messiah." So here we have three terms with one meaning: Christ, Messiah, Anointed. In Biblical times ointment was used widely for medical purposes, as suggested by the beloved psalm, "Thou anointest my head with oil." Perhaps for this reason, anointment was part of the ceremony for ordaining a priest, or commissioning a prophet, or crowning a king. It was an enacted prayer that God would grant the person health and strength to fulfill his responsibilities.

A strain of prediction runs through the Old Testament, about God's coming representative on earth. He is first mentioned when the Lord speaks to the serpent in the Garden, foretelling that the seed of the woman "shall bruise your head, and you shall bruise his heel." Before Jesus' time, the Hebrew community called this representative-to-be the Messiah. As the Old Testament develops, so does the picture of the future Christ, or Messiah, or Anointed.

When Jesus was born, the Hebrew people were anticipating the Christ. Some held the most exalted ideas about the coming Messiah, and some thought of Him as only a military leader who would free the Jews from Rome. Peter showed that he belonged with the former group, when he said to Jesus, "You are the Christ, the Son of the living God." And ever since, this has been the faith of the Christian Church: that Jesus, the special representative of God, is, in some way that nobody begins to understand, linked with the heavenly Father. It took time and Christian experience to assimilate this idea, which today we call the Incarnation, or the embodiment of God. Church councils at Nicea, Constantinople, and Chalcedon tried — and failed — to explain it. They did not give the Christian answer; instead they gave marvelously precise statements of the question. The clearest expression the idea ever received came from Thomas the doubter, who knelt before Christ and said, "My Lord and my God."

JESUS ACCEPTS THE ANSWER

If I were to come to you, bowing low and saying, "Queen Elizabeth, I presume?" you would immediately set me right. You are not Queen Elizabeth, and a normally decent person will reject honors to which he is not entitled. A confidence man allows others to think more highly about him than the facts would justify. The rest of us try not to be hypocrites. Jesus, the teacher of righteousness, to whom people by the hundred million look for moral guidance, allowed Peter to call Him "the Christ, the Son of the living God." The isolated fact that Peter said this is not significant. Peter was mistaken frequently. Sometimes he blurted out more than he really meant. It is significant that Jesus accepted the title.

Not only did Jesus accept the title "Christ, the Son of the living God," He said that God had led Peter to this statement of faith. "Blessed are you, Simon Bar-Jonah — [that means Simon Johnson] — for flesh and blood has not revealed this to you, but my Father who is in heaven." And right here, at the moment when the Church was founded, Jesus draws the line between information and faith. You can acquire necessary and important information about Jesus from the encyclopedia. No intelligent person would make any decisions about Jesus without first securing all the information he can get.

But Peter had no more information about Jesus after he declared his faith than he did before. Faith is what you do with the information. And Jesus said that Christian faith is not just information — which we can get from one another — faith is, in some sense, a gift from God.

As Christians today anxiously examine the Church's place in the world, we ought to draw two important conclusions from its founding. First, the Lord founded the Church, not on the faith of a theological expert, but rather on that of a theological weakling. Most Christians today can see themselves mirrored more clearly in Simon Peter than in any other New Testament person. We ought likewise to notice where Jesus founded the Church, not in the holy city Jerusalem, but in a luxurious holiday resort where the surroundings denied almost everything that Jesus proclaimed.

JESUS FOUNDS THE CHURCH

Unhappily, the Church today is divided about the meaning of a relative pronoun, "this." Jesus accepted Peter's declaration and said, with one of the plays on words that He loved, "I tell you, you are Peter." This was a nickname, meaning "Rock," that Jesus applied when first they met to the most un-rock-like man you could imagine. A rock stays put. Simon did not. He was always changing his mind, always shifting from here to there. But Jesus, who gave the ironical nickname to a man of quicksand, knew what He was doing. A lifetime of faith gradually solidified the quicksand.

Up to this point, the Protestant and the Roman Catholic are in complete agreement. From this point on, we must disagree (and I rejoice that we are today expressing our disagreement in charity, each recognizing that the other is sincere, if mistaken).

As a usual thing, when you employ the elusive word "this," you refer to the thing you have just been talking about. Jesus and Peter have just been talking about the faith that Jesus Christ is the Son of God. And the Lord says, "I tell you, you are a rock, and on this rock I will build my Church." A person, approaching the sentence without presuppositions, would understand "this" as the faith that is under discussion.

Our Roman Catholic friends, however, understand the relative pronoun in a different way. They say that Jesus addressed Simon, ". . . and I tell you, you are Peter." Then, turning to the other disciples, he pointed to Peter and said, "On this rock I will build my Church." So, they say, He made Peter the first head of the Church, entrusting to him the keys of the Kingdom, which have been transmitted to each successive pope.

It is almost beyond question that Peter went to Rome, where he served as bishop — the Greek for overseer — of the Church. It is history that spiritual authority gradually accrued to the bishop in the capital city, who was known affectionately as "papa," hence our word "pope." During the Middle Ages the struggle between popes and emperors culminated in an apparent victory for the Church, when the pope forced the emperor to wait three days, barefoot, in the snow at Canossa, to sue for a pardon. The development of the papacy led to the Vatican Council of 1870 at which it was declared that the pope, not only Pius IX but every pope before and after his time, is divinely guarded against error when speaking officially about a matter of faith or morals. The doctrine is not so crass as many Protestants try to make it, but still it provides a major obstacle to the Church union for which many of us — Protestants and Roman Catholics alike — are praying.

William L. Sullivan was a Roman Catholic priest who began to examine the infallibility of the pope, first sympathetically, then critically, and finally decided that he must break with Rome because he could not accept this dogma. I quote the most meaningful paragraph — to me — in Dr. Sullivan's autobiography.

> If the Pope was held infallible from the beginning, the early Fathers who wrote so largely upon the faith, and whose authority stands so high as the standard of faith, would witness to the fact. But they do not. As the opposition bishops repeatedly said at the Council, not a single Father of the Church, Greek or Latin, and not a single General Council attributes infallibility to the Pope alone. Even on the fundamental Scriptural support of the papal claims, the text in which Jesus calls Simon a rock on which He builds

His Church, and gives to Peter the keys of the kingdom, only seventeen of the Fathers say that, in these words, the Church was built on Peter; but forty-four declare that the rock was Peter's faith in the divinity of the Lord — an extraordinary state of affairs if those early teachers knew of the infallibility of Peter's successor. Could they have been so silent if they knew anything about the dogma?

We Protestants highly respect Simon Peter and all other leaders in the Church, ancient and modern, but we believe that the Church is built, not upon Peter as a man, but upon Peter's faith which we share. If we may accept Dr. Sullivan's count, we agree with three-fourths of early Church fathers who wrote about the matter.

On "this" rock Jesus Christ, the Son of God, founded His "Church." The New Testament word is *ecclesia* (those who are called out). The ancient Athenian *ecclesia* was the legislative and judicial assembly comprising all citizens in good standing. In cases of urgent gravity, six thousand citizens must be present to vote. The Greek Old Testament uses *ecclesia* to translate the Hebrew *qahal*, which, derived from a root "to summon," means the "assembly" or "congregation." The emphasis is upon God's "call" to which the *qahal* or *ecclesia* answers. The word is inclusive; God "calls" the whole people "out" from their homes and farms and shops to serve Him.

Our English word has its own complex history. "Church" began with the Greek adjective *kuriakos*, "belonging to the Lord." The Greek word for "lord," *kurios*, was a sign of respect directed to almost any gentleman. It would have been almost unthinkable not to use the title in speaking to or about Jesus. But the same word in the Greek Old Testament expresses the sacred name of God (what today we call Jehovah or Yahweh.) So in the New Testament the Savior is *kurios* in both senses of the term. An adjective "belonging to the Lord" was *kuriakos*. Our fathers referred to the *ecclesia* as the *kuriakos*. And so, by traceable steps, we find the Anglo-Saxon *cyrice* or *circe*. A shift of consonants, no one knows why, changed the word to Middle English *chirche*, with which our *church* is practically identical.

The rich history of two related words gives the essential

ideas about the Church. God calls all the people. Those who respond form the assembly belonging to the Lord. This is what "church" has meant in the past. Far more important, as far as you are concerned, is what it means in your life.

THE GATES OF HELL

Contemporary literature and drama take a dim view of the Church. When, on rare occasions, a Christian is pictured as a masculine figure, genuinely fighting for what he believes, almost invariably the Church is pictured as the chief millstone about his neck. Jesus, who founded the Church, said in the charter-deed, "The gates of hell shall not prevail against it." This was an idiomatic Hebrew expression, found in Isaiah, the Book of the Maccabees, and the Wisdom Literature. Modern English translations read, "the powers of death" or something of the sort, which is perhaps a little more accurate, but a great deal less colorful. Jesus loved the colorful phrase; why should we reject it?

I suppose I was about eight years old when the Savior's words about the gates of hell registered with me. I pictured what the Lord was talking about. The gates of hell would come up to the Church and bang away for a while, then they would get tired and go away. I have needed to change many theological opinions since passing my ninth birthday. For one thing, how would you batter down anything with a gate? It is the wrong size and shape.

Gradually it seeped into my consciousness that I had the figure of speech all wrong. Jesus isn't talking about the Church withstanding the assault from hell. Rather He means that hell will crumble before the Church. In Jesus' time a major city was surrounded by a wall in which were hung massive gates that would be closed at night and whenever attack threatened. Since the gate was the most vulnerable part of the city's defense, the general would usually center his attack on it. Jesus knew, at least as well as we do, that the forces of evil are intelligently organized and capable of long-continued defense. He set His Church to work, battering down these defenses.

THE KEYS

Then Jesus said to Peter, "I will give you the keys of the kingdom of heaven, and whatever you loose on earth shall be loosed in heaven." A. J. Cronin entitled his novel *The Keys of the Kingdom,* and everyone knew that this book concerns the pope. So popular theology, even among Protestants, has conceded this particular verse to the Roman Catholics, who have not been reluctant to accept it. On the other occasions when Jesus talks about the power to bind and to loose, He addresses the entire Church. Here He speaks to Peter, the man who has just confessed his faith in the divine Son of God, as representative of the other disciples who will join in the declaration. I cannot believe that by these few words Jesus intended to found the historic papacy, but at the same moment, I must say that Jesus placed a far greater importance upon the organized fellowship of the faithful than does the contemporary Protestant. Our emphasis upon individual piety leads us to treat the Church as a genial assembly of pleasant people who happen to enjoy religion; our Lord thought it more important.

Jesus says, "I will give you the keys." He is pointing ahead to a time when the Master of the house has left for an extended journey, as He pictured it in several parables, leaving the servants in charge. He refers to a familiar passage in Isaiah, where God chooses Eliakim to be chief steward over King Hezekiah's household, and says to Shebna, the steward who has been unfaithful:

> I will call my servant Eliakim . . . and I will clothe him with your robe, and will bind your girdle on him, and will commit your authority to his hand; and he shall be a father to the inhabitants of Jerusalem and to the house of Judah. And I will place on his shoulder the key of the house of David; he shall open, and none shall shut; and he shall shut, and none shall open.
>
> Isaiah 22:20-23.

The key is a symbol for the authority to decide who shall enter and who shall be excluded from the house.

The phrase about binding and loosing was likewise familiar to the disciples, who had heard it in their synagogues from childhood. It means forbidding and allowing, with particular reference to the interpretation of Scripture. The Savior entrusts to His Church the task of interpreting God's will to society. This is genuine authority, like that of admitting and excluding, but it is delegated authority. Peter, with the other disciples, is to be a "steward," not master of the house.

Jesus is not talking on this occasion about the forgiveness of sins. On another occasion, though, the Lord said to his disciples — not to Peter individually —

> As the Father has sent me, even so I send you. . . .Receive the Holy Spirit. If you forgive the sins of any, they are forgiven; if you retain the sins of any, they are retained.
>
> John 20:20.

On these meaningful words the Roman Catholics have built the Sacrament of Penance. The Reformers, over-reacting against abuses of this sacramental act, left us in the curious position where some Protestants seem to think that the Church does not enter the picture of divine forgiveness. To whom, but the Church, did our Savior deliver those chill words about retaining sin? Our failures to forgive have left modern society wallowing in its guilt.

As a pastor I spend much of my time hearing confessions and pronouncing God's forgiveness. I do not use a confessional booth, and the confessions I hear are usually more rambling and disjointed than those a Roman Catholic priest hears. But these are outward and trivial differences. The big difference is that I say, "God forgives you," while my friend the priest says, "I forgive you" (*te absolvo*). Yet we two are not quite so far apart as seems to be the case. The Roman Catholic priest does not claim absolute power to forgive. When a person makes a "bad confession," usually by keeping his fingers crossed about continuing the sin, the priest in all sincerity pronounces the absolution, but the sin is not considered to be forgiven. The sinner has not fulfilled the conditions, and the priest claims no power to forgive what God has not forgiven.

Protestants have had several centuries to think the matter over, and we seem to be agreeing upon the psychological value of a spoken confession into a human ear, plus the value of systematic self-investigation with the help of a sympathetic counsellor. If one may judge by the written reports, the Protestant minister a century ago considered himself primarily a preacher, while the minister today considers himself primarily a counsellor.

God has summoned the whole world to assemble at the Cross of Christ. Many have answered the call, and confessed that Jesus is the Christ, the Son of the living God. These people compose the Church, which has the authority to determine who is and who is not a Christian, to interpret the Holy Scripture, and to say under what conditions a sin is forgiven. Modern novelists know what is wrong with the Church. So do you. So do I. So does God. Even so, the divine Savior entrusted to this earthly institution the task of battering down the gates of hell.

2
THE BODY OF CHRIST
I Corinthians 12:12-27

I Corinthians 12:12-27

As the body is one and has many members, and all the members of the body, though many, are one body, so it is with Christ. For by one Spirit we were all baptized into one body — Jews or Greeks, slaves or free — and all were made to drink of one Spirit.

For the body does not consist of one member but of many. If the foot should say, "Because I am not a hand, I do not belong to the body," that would not make it any less a part of the body. And if the ear should say, "Because I am not an eye, I do not belong to the body," that would not make it any less a part of the body. If the whole body were an eye, where would be the hearing? If the whole body were an ear, where would be the sense of smell? But as it is, God arranged the organs in the body, each one of them, as he chose. If all were a single organ, where would the body be? As it is, there are many parts, yet one body. The eye cannot say to the hand, "I have no need of you," nor again the head to the feet, "I have no need of you." On the contrary, the parts of the body which seem to be weaker are indispensable, and those parts of the body which we think less honorable we invest with the greater honor, and our unpresentable parts are treated with greater modesty, which our more presentable parts do not require. But God has so adjusted the body, giving the greater honor to the inferior part, that there may be no discord in the body, but that the members may have the same care for one another. If one member suffers, all suffer together; if one member is honored, all rejoice together.

Now you are the body of Christ and individually members of it.

THE BODY OF CHRIST

I Corinthians 12:12-27

Today and next week I want to think with you about two statements in the New Testament that, at first, sound alike, but actually are quite different. This morning: "The Church is the Body of Christ." Next week: "Your body is the temple of the Holy Spirit." Next week we shall be thinking about a figure of speech. Today we are examining a statement of fact.

THE BODY OF CHRIST

Nineteen centuries ago, the divine Savior walked about on earth in a body much like yours. He needed food and shelter and sleep. He enjoyed a good dinner and He grew discouraged when He was tired — just like you. His body was subject to every disease that threatens you. And finally He died; He bled to death. But Christians have always insisted that death was not the end. In some manner far beyond our understanding He rose from the dead and He lives today. We pray to Him, up in heaven. Yet we believe likewise that He walks and talks on earth today in a body that we call the Church. This is no figure of speech. The Church is, in every literal sense, the Body of Christ.

Try something a little more familiar. "General Electric is a corporation." You could not very well argue with the statement. General Electric is a group of people who are banded together to produce and distribute electrical apparatus. These different people contribute their individual skills to a task too great for any one to accomplish by himself.

A crack design engineer might be a poor salesman. The best salesman in the whole corporation might make a poor auditor. An auditor who knows everything about finance might be totally unable to wind an armature. Many different people contribute diverse skills to General Electric. The similarity to the Church is obvious; so we call ourselves the Body of Christ, and we call General Electric a corporation, a Latin word meaning body. The business world borrowed from the Church the idea of corporation, which is a group of people working as one to achieve a stated purpose.

The resemblance between Church and corporation is great; the difference likewise is great. Significantly, the Bible never mentions the body of Christians; only the Body of Christ. A corporation consists of the people who form it; remove them and there's nothing left. In contrast, the unremovable Christ calls us to membership in His Body. We are in the Church of our own will, but we are not simply a human community with an exalted purpose. We are a human community called together by Christ. Legally, a corporation is a fictitious person. Christ is no fiction; He is *the* Person, and we are members of His Body.

We spend so much time stoking our bodies and keeping them adequately draped that we rarely stop to ask what a body is for. You can get lost down all sorts of philosophic by-paths answering the question; but two answers, I believe, are beyond argument: your body enables me to recognize you as you, and your body enables you to act.

Within the vast conglomeration called humanity you are an individual. I can pick you out by your face, your voice, the way you walk. Your body distinguishes you as yourself. You comb your hair in the morning, staring bleakly at the mirror. You might well pause to recognize that you are surveying what others see of Christ. You are part of His body. The thought should be sobering.

Mr. Altizer, who recently discovered that God is dead, has remarked trenchantly, "The identification of Christianity with the Christian Church may well be the major source of the troubles that now beset the Christian faith." Mr. Altizer has been badly mistaken about some important matters; in this he could be correct. The world listens to the shrill bickering

that emanates from Zion, shakes its head sadly and looks elsewhere for salvation. As people say on Madison Avenue, "The
Church doesn't have a good image today." Yet a Person
much wiser than any of His critics founded the Church upon
the faith that exists in human hearts. He ordained people
— bull-headed, cantankerous, stubborn people — to be Church
members. He knew we're hard to get along with; that's why
we need the Church.

Paul wrote the Corinthians to meet a practical crisis within
the congregation: Christians were standing apart and skillfully hurling theological brick-bats at one another. Further,
the congregation was infected with immorality so garish that
it would cause raised eyebrows even on Miami Beach. The
contemporary image of the Church is bad, but that in Corinth
was worse when the Apostle called his brother-Christians the
Body of Christ. The world gets a poor impression of Christ
from us; even so, sometimes the real message gets across.

I have read about people who were converted by reading
the Gospel according to St. Luke, but I have yet to meet such
a person. Everyone who has told me about his own conver-
sion came into Christian faith through a living Christian from
whom he caught the Spirit of Christ. Wherever an individual
radiates this Spirit, there is the Church that matters, and
there is the Body of Christ. Frequently I think the Lord
might have presented Christianity to the world in a more
attractive package than the Church:

> With a scornful wonder men see her sore oppressed,
> By schisms rent asunder, by heresies distressed.

Yet God has chosen to reveal Christ to the world chiefly
through our clumsy hands and blundering lips.

Your body enables you to act. So it is with the Body of
Christ. Of course, you can reach far beyond your physical
limitations. You write to a mail-order house in Chicago.
After the letter leaves your hands you no longer have any
physical control over it. Perhaps fifty other people must
handle the letter and the resulting order before the goods
you want return to you. So Christ is not limited by what His
Church does on earth. If it is true that in some miraculous

sense God was in Christ, then He was at work on earth ages before He founded the Church, and He controls every molecule today. He is present in the lives even of those who most violently reject Him. Christ can work through any individual or organization to achieve His purpose.

It calls for no rejoicing by the Church that others have outdone us in serving Christ: trade unions, public schools, governmental agencies, industrial corporations, and civil rights organizations have frequently shown more deep Christ-like concern for the poor, the weak, and the oppressed than we have.

Some have even called Communism a Christian heresy with God left out. Karl Marx certainly adopted social ideas from Jesus without giving credit to the Author. Where did Karl Marx hear the gospel, where but through the Church he so much despised? Even when your actions go beyond your body — as in sending that order to Chicago — the action begins when your mind telegraphs an instruction to your fingers. Christ works beyond the earthly organization called the Church, yet this is His Body in the world to do His will. As a usual thing He begins His redeeming work on earth through us.

MEMBERSHIP IN THE BODY

If you will read carefully what the Apostle says about the Body of Christ, you will discover that he had an intensely practical reason for saying it. He was not concerned primarily to give us another way of thinking about the Church, but to help Christians act like Christians. His emphasis is not so much upon the body as on the members. The other day I looked up "member" in my dictionary, and found that, according to Mr. Webster, the Biblical word is obsolete English. What the Bible calls a "member" we now call an "organ." I don't know that we have contributed much to human progress by changing a word. Let's stick with the old term for today.

We think about membership today as taking part in an organization's activities. The term originally meant being a hand, a foot, an eye, or some other part of the body. Your bodily members have much in common; the chromosome structure in the different parts binds you together as one. But the unity that is you consists of many differences without which you would be an inert blob of protoplasm. Your left arm is not your right arm. Your left hand differs from your right hand. Both differ greatly from your left foot. The difference between foot and ear is fantastic.

Your members work together to do your will. You have many needs which different bodily organs meet by performing their different functions. Breathing is not seeing. Seeing is not eating. Eating is not walking. Yet these different activities depend on one another.

If the Church is the Body of Christ we should not be surprised that the members differ from one another. Christ meets different needs through different members of His Body. Here the need is hunger, there it is disease, there it is crime, and there it is such abundance that God is crowded out, but underlying each visible symptom is the same fundamental need for Christ. One person can't meet every need; that's why the Church has many members.

The needs may be numbered by the million. Church members likewise are numbered by the million. As we individuals tackle individual needs, administering the cup of cold water in Christ's Name, we are acting effectually as members of His Body.

> To one is given through the Spirit the utterance of wisdom, to another the utterance of knowledge according to the same Spirit, to another faith by the same Spirit, to another gifts of healing by the same Spirit, to another the working of miracles, to another prophecy, to another the ability to distinguish between spirits, to another various kinds of tongues, to another the interpretation of tongues. All these are inspired by one and the same Spirit, who apportions to each one individually as He wills.
>
> I Corinthians 12:18-11.

As Paul has told us, we differ from one another because God made us different. He did so because many needs exist in the world and different people meet them in different ways. One-half the human race is ill equipped for motherhood, for example.

God made us different. I know a man who is splendid in working with young people, yet his booming exuberance is totally exhausting to the aged. God, who equipped him for one valuable type of service, has equipped others for the quiet, gentle ministry to His elderly children. You simply do not reach the intellectual skeptic with the same approach that reaches the bar-fly. A person who might successfully reach one might repel the other. We need each other if we are to be the Church.

HANDS AND KNEES

An unhappy division exists in the Church today between the sons of Mary and the sons of Martha. Martha, you recall, was the Christian activist, always rushing about, doing something. She was Christ's hand. And Mary, you recall, was the Christian pietist, praying, thinking, being rather than doing. She was the knees of Christ. When Martha came bustling up to our Lord and said, "Tell that lazy sister of mine to stir her stumps," Jesus said to her,

> Martha, Martha, you are anxious and troubled about many things, one thing is needful. Mary has chosen the good portion, which shall not be taken away from her.
>
> Luke 10:41.

Just one moment: let us not decide that the Church belongs to Mary, and cast the sons of Martha into outer darkness. The Bible tells us that Jesus loved Martha and Mary and Lazarus, whose chief function in the Biblical narrative is to warn us against giving up quite so readily; mere death cannot stop Christ. Jesus loved Martha, the activist. Jesus loved Mary, the pietist. And Jesus loved Lazarus, who was still asleep.

The Church contains many whom God has called to social action. The Church contains many whom God has called to the contemplative life. (And the Church likewise contains many who, like Lazarus, seem to us beyond responding to any call.) To hear the activists and the pietists talking about one another, you might never guess they belong to the same Body, and this is exactly the situation that Paul was addressing in Corinth.

> The eye cannot say to the hand, "I have no need of you,"
> nor again the head to the feet, "I have no need of you."
> On the contrary, the parts of the body which seem to be
> weaker are indispensable.
>
> I Corinthians 12:21-22.

We hands and we knees require one another.

Picture the Christian activist, shivering beside a low fire on the picket-line, while his feet ache dismally. You can appreciate that he grows a bit irritated with his brother Christian whom God has called to the easy life, contemplating at convenient hours of the day. His irritation has long antecedents, going back to Martha. But he is badly mistaken about one thing. Prayer is not easy. Prayer is about the hardest work — and the most important work — in which a Christian can engage. I do not propose to abandon public or private worship so that we can all march on Selma.

I have read learned diatribes by Christian activists against their brothers who are less active. When it comes to venom, they pale into nothing beside the pious scorn of the pietists. I know Christians who believe, sincerely, that their brothers are mistaken in trying to correct specific social evils. As if one mistake were not enough, they proceed to smear every one who is active in social causes. You would think that while they were on their knees in prayer they might remember something about charity, which they might even extend to their brother Christians.

THE BODY OF CHRIST AND THE EXAMPLE OF JESUS

I serve with our Presbytery's Committee on Candidates. One day we were talking with a young man who is thinking seriously about the ministry. He was expressing deep and Christ-like concern about the tragic needs that exist in our world. Then he began to express some doubts about his entering the ministry, and the chief of these was, "The Church just doesn't seem interested in meeting the needs." It was precisely concern for similar needs as they existed thirty years ago that led me into a Church vocation. My belief that the Church is better able to tackle human need than any other organization in society led me where I am.

I still hold to this belief, though it gets badly shaken when people with obvious devotion to Christ and His gospel advocate a course of action that scuttles what Christ stood for.

The *Wall Street Journal*, which does not usually speak for the left wing, recently published a long, thoughtful article about the shortage of applicants for the clergy. The conclusion is that strong men are avoiding the ministry because the Church is not sufficiently involved in the heartache of modern society — and the majority of members want it that way. The article says:

> Youths who feel strongly an urge to correct racial wrongs, for example, are unconvinced, rightly or wrongly, that the church is the place to do it. . . . Some would-be clergymen appear to find more scope for their idealism in social or Government work. The Peace Corps says at least 120 seminary graduates have gone into its overseas technical assistance programs. The Office of Economic Opportunity, which runs the Federal anti-poverty program, adds that a "large number" of former ministers run agencies it supports.

Shall we reserve the Church for those who are passionately concerned about doctrine, while those who care about people serve God elsewhere? The ancient Pharisees were passionate about doctrinal matters, and Jesus thought their faith somewhat lacking.

Many contemporary pietists seem to feel that if the Church is seriously involved in the issues of the day somehow this interest detracts from our primary responsibility, which is the relationship of the individual to Almighty God. I cannot follow them. Such concern is the direct expression of my personal commitment to Christ, and I think of yours also. If concern leads to political action, can you suggest where the Spirit of Christ is more needed than in politics?

The New Testament is painfully clear that Jesus cared about people and their needs. He cared when they were hungry, sick, lonely, or discriminated against. He did what He could to alleviate human misery. He got so involved with the political machinery of His time that He was crucified. There were two other courses open to Him: greasily accepting the status quo with the Herodians, or revolutionary violence with the Zealots. He rejected both. (So should your Church.) The political decisions in Palestine were made by a Roman Procurator whose instructions came from Rome, not from a mandate of the Palestinian people. There were no polls for Jesus to go to, no legislators to whom He could write.

Turn back to your Old Testament and you will find religious leaders, in a different set of circumstances, overthrowing kings, smashing unjust laws, denouncing foreign policy, and legislating about weights and measures. They thought their faith demanded such activity.

The Church has always been up to the neck in the issues of the day, but we easily forget the past. There is nothing quite so soporific as yesterday's burning issue. It is hard to reconstruct the passion that once flamed after a matter has been taken for granted.

The Church has, in times past (and present) been deeply and wrongly involved in politics. The mediaeval Spanish archbishops had their own private armies, and on at least one occasion, during the dispute about the succession of Ferdinand and Isabella, two of them were at war with one another, doubtless to the glory of God. And in Hitler's time the "German Christians" became so enmeshed in political machinery that they could no longer speak independently for Christ. I do not defend this sort of involvement. But when a particular evil can be corrected the Church is obligated to do what it can, under existing circumstances, to overcome evil with good.

> What does it profit . . . if a man says he has faith but has not works? Can his faith save him? If a brother or sister is ill-clad and in lack of daily food, and one of you say to them, "Go in peace, be warmed and filled," without giving them the things needed for the body, what does it profit?
>
> James 2:14-16.

Techniques for feeding the hungry brother vary. Once it meant leaving the corners of a field unharvested. On another occasion it meant a cash offering which Paul carried to Jerusalem. If today it means prodding the legislature, the motive is the same and the goal is the same. The brother needs to eat.

The chief trouble with the so-called welfare state is that we have fossilized emergency procedures and taught people to depend on the dole. The tragedy is not that Christians have cared too much about the poor; we have cared too little. We have urged the government to feed them, and have forgotten that man does not live by bread alone. Government cannot love — that's supposed to be our job, and we haven't done it very well.

Recently a friend came waving a printed sermon under my nose and bellowed, "Why can't the Church preach the truth like this, instead of always meddling in politics?" The sermon was a feebly-thought but eloquently-spoken attack on the welfare state, based more or less on the text, "If any one will not work, let him not eat" (II Thessalonians 3:10). (The thought in question, of course, is central to Karl Marx's attack on capitalism, under which some who do not work are enabled to eat remarkably well.) My friend does not object when the Church agrees with him about political matters, but he is pained if the Church asks him to prod his own conscience about his attitude toward the poor, the minorities, the obligations of wealth, and Christ's way to overcome Communism.

If any Christian is so involved in the world's affairs that he has lost sight of his eternal goal, he is badly mistaken and should be reminded, in love, that we have here no continuing city. Such a mistake — which genuinely exists — in no way justifies the opposite error, making our faith so spiritual that we can ignore the cry of human pain. Christ's Kingdom is not of this world, but He cared and still cares about the hungry people who live here.

What hits me the hardest in current attacks on the Church is that our critics no longer think Christianity worth denouncing. They believe that the Church has sold out to the desire for safety and security, that we are not really concerned about the things that Jesus was concerned about. We just want to be left alone to mumble our prayers in comfort. The attacks that hurt are not about our actions (some of which have been mistaken) but about our cowardly failures to act.

The chief weakness in Christian activism today is a lack of contemplation leading up to the act. And the chief weakness in

Christian pietism is a lack of concrete earthly goals. Jesus thought that before the five thousand could reach their eternal home, they might well have a bite to eat on the way.

Only a few days ago I talked with a young Christian who was simply stunned by a meeting he had attended, at which older Christians were disagreeing heartily with some plans that others were making to relieve human need in slum areas. My young friend said, "I have never heard such hate in human voices, and all the time they were talking about love. These people think that everyone who is trying to help anyone is a Communist. What's the matter with the Church?"

The Church has exactly the same trouble we have always had. The members are people, not archangels. Christ laid His good life down because people need help. He called us sinners to become members of His Body, and He tries to make us worthy of the privilege that is ours. All this was true in Corinth. All this is true today. Paul's message is that we members in the Body of Christ must learn each to make his individual contribution to the Church's health, and each to respect his brother Christian who is making a different kind of contribution. Our brothers may well be mistaken in their tactics. If so, they need our love and understanding, not our scorn. Christ's way is risky. But I can't think of a better place to practice it than within His earthly Body.

3

THE TEMPLE OF THE HOLY SPIRIT

I Corinthians 6:19-20; Isaiah 6:1-8

I Corinthians 6:19-20

Do you not know that your body is a temple of the Holy Spirit within you, which you have from God? You are not your own; you were bought with a price. So glorify God in your body.

Isaiah 6:1-8

In the year that King Uzziah died I saw the Lord sitting upon a throne, high and lifted up; and his train filled the temple. Above him stood the seraphim; each had six wings: with two he covered his face, and with two he covered his feet, and with two he flew. And one called to another and said:

> "Holy, holy, holy is the Lord of hosts;
> the whole earth is full of his glory."

And the foundations of the thresholds shook at the voice of him who called, and the house was filled with smoke. And I said: "Woe is me! For I am lost; for I am a man of unclean lips, and I dwell in the midst of a people of unclean lips; for my eyes have seen the King, the Lord of hosts!" Then flew one of the seraphim to me, having in his hand a burning coal which he had taken with tongs from the altar. And he touched my mouth, and said: "Behold, this has touched your lips; your guilt is taken away, and your sin forgiven." And I heard the voice of the Lord saying, "Whom shall I send, and who will go for us?" Then I said, "Here I am! Send me."

3

THE TEMPLE OF THE HOLY SPIRIT

I Corinthians 6:19-20; Isaiah 6:1-8

You are a member in the body of Christ when you are met with your fellow Christians at public worship on Sunday. You are just as much a member in the Body of Christ on Friday when you are earning your daily bread, or whatever you do on Friday. Sometimes the Church is gathered, sometimes the Church is dispersed. Today we are thinking about the Church dispersed throughout the community, and more particularly about you as a member of the Church.

THE TEMPLE

Last Wednesday a lovely girl, sixteen or seventeen, said, "You told us Sunday that our bodies are the temple of the Holy Spirit."

I said, "I'm glad someone was listening."

She said, "Well, it sounds silly to me. What does it mean?"

I explained that a lot of important ideas sound a little odd until you get used to them, and I assured her that the word "body" means just exactly what it usually means: the physical organism that people clothe and feed, that has arms and legs and lungs. The Bible doesn't offer much consolation to those who want their faith to be a nice-Nellie affair having nothing to do with hunger and thirst and sexual drives. Our faith is for people who live in bodies that get sick and lead them into temptation. And our faith teaches us to call these bodies the temple of the Holy Spirit.

She said, "It still doesn't make any sense."

So I asked, "What's the Temple?"

She said, "That was the place where the Jewish people used to worship. It was sort of like our Church building."

I said, "Go to the head of the class. And who is the Holy Spirit?"

She said, "I haven't forgotten everything we learned in Communicants' Class. Do you want the whole answer, or will you settle if I say that's one of the ways we speak about God?"

I said, "I'll settle. Your body is the Church building where you worship God. Is that any better?"

She answered, "Not a bit."

So I said, "I pay a fantastic lot of taxes to support that school you go to. Now let's see if I'm getting my money's worth. I'm your English teacher, and here's the examination question: *Your body is the temple of the Holy Spirit. Comment.*"

She thought this over for a minute and said, "It's a metaphor, which means thinking about one thing in terms of another thing because of some real or imagined resemblance. The Temple was a place where people worshiped God. My body is a place I can't get away from. Does Paul mean that I ought to be worshiping God wherever I am?"

I can't tell you how happy I was with the conversation, and not only because the tax-payer is getting his money's worth. I spend so much time talking with people who are trying to evade Christianity that it's a real shock of pleasure to meet someone who wants to examine the heart of Christian conduct, and I don't mind a bit if people say out loud that some Biblical thoughts are hard to grasp. (Neither, I believe, does the heavenly Father object.)

When Paul wrote to the Corinthians the Temple building stood in Jerusalem. An educated guess is that the Temple was about 175 feet long, 80 feet wide, and 3 stories high. It stood on stone foundations. Its sides were massive walls. On top it had a roof. Leading up to the entrance were steps. The priests entered it through a door. That is, the Temple was similar to any other large building in most respects. It was a material structure in a material world, built of wood and stone by carpenters and masons. The Temple differed from other buildings in its purpose. It was a place where people worshiped Almighty God.

As my young friend suggested, we can think about the ancient Temple by examining our Church building today. The many differences between them do not concern us now. Temple and Church building alike are material structures, dedicated to a spiritual purpose.

In our own Church we find that we must always be taking care of the building. Not long ago the roof wore out and required some amazingly expensive repairs. Then the plumbing sprang a costly leak. Windows frequently break. It has been said that if you plant a white fence post in the ground you must take care of it or shortly you will have a dirty brown fence post, and not long after that no fence post at all. The Church building is far more complex than a fence post. We must take time, thought, and money to keep it ready for worship, as our fathers did with the ancient Temple.

Our Church building is dedicated to a purpose, which Isaiah has described to perfection: the personal encounter with God that we call worship. Isaiah encountered God. He honestly faced himself, and declared to God what was wrong in his life. God cleansed him and offered him a duty. And Isaiah accepted the duty. This — whenever and wherever and however it happens — is worship.

YOUR BODY

Your body contains the same kind of chemicals that go into a building. Calcium is calcium, whether in your bones or in cement. Your body is a material structure in this material world. The great difference between your body and this building is that God has given you the miracle of life. The question before us is what you are doing with the gift.

Your body is always in motion. On Sundays when you are gathered with the congregation it is relatively easy to realize that your chief business in life is worship. On Tuesday afternoon, when the Church is dispersed in the world that crucified our Lord, it is sometimes difficult to remember. Gathered or dispersed, the Church is one. In the company of other Christians or away from your fellow Christians you are a member of the Body of Christ whenever and wherever

and however you are worshiping Him, or, in other words,
your body is a temple of Christ's Spirit.

WORSHIP AND HUMDRUM

We spend most of our time in ways that do not look especially worshipful: eating, sleeping, earning a living, shop-
ping for groceries, and washing the dirty clothes. Yet without this humdrum there can be little worship. Go without
water for a day, and God's glory will not be uppermost in
your mind.

As I have said, if we hope to worship God in this building
we do so in part by taking care of it with a mop and paint
brush. Sometimes Christians have attempted to worship God
by almost destroying their bodies. They have starved themselves to delirium; they have slept on spikes; and, worst
of all, they have acted as if there is something shameful
about the miracle by which God continues human life. Christian faith will not have it so.

The Word became flesh. Jesus came to the world not a
disembodied spirit but a squalling infant. His infant lips
suckled His mother's breast. He grew with a ravenous teen-
ager's appetite. As a man He knew every physical need
and every emotion that the heavenly Father built into you.
His divine life was lived amid all the complexities, tensions
and contradictions that you and I know.

Our heavenly Father invented the body. He invented every human need, and He invented the right way to fulfill
each need. You make your body the temple of the Holy
Spirit, in part, by meeting human need in a Christian way.

Jesus said, "As you did it to one of the least of these, my
brethren, you did it to me." That is, if you meet a neighbor
who has no shoes, and take him to the shoe-store to buy
him what he needs, you have come face to face with Christ,
which is the heart of Christian worship.

What happens when you buy yourself a pair of shoes?
Aren't you one of God's children. He created your feet. He
knows that people who live in crowded cities need foot pro-
tection and support. Shouldn't it be worship when you fulfill
your God-given needs? You would find it hard to worship in

this building if we didn't take good care of it. Similarly you must care for your basic physical needs in order to carry on spiritual life. Each trip to the shoe-store ought to be worship.

Almighty God invented hunger. Our Saviour taught us to ask the heavenly Father for daily bread. At the table we Christians bow and thank the Giver for His gift; thus crunching into a watermelon ought to be an act of worship. (Everything we do in the temple of the Holy Spirit ought to be worship.) Some people center their lives around the table. Instead of eating to live, they live to eat, and so they destroy the temple of the Holy Spirit with their teeth. Yet eating remains good until man makes it bad.

Our heavenly Father invented work. The third chapter in the Bible tells that the gift of work began God's plan for our salvation. Doing well what your hand finds to do is integral to Christian living. Yet we all know people who have made a god out of work, who treat their bodies as money-making machines.

Our heavenly Father gave us the gift of love. One of the most sacred and holy acts of worship that we perform here is joining a man and a woman in marriage as they express their love of God through their love for one another. Your Pastor likewise spends many heartbreaking hours dealing with people who thought they knew more about love than God does. They followed their bodily desires and not the wisdom of Christ. It is the fashion now-a-days to urge that we express our sexual lusts. The people who do the urging do not seem to look beyond the pleasure of the moment (which can be intensely pleasurable) to the grief that follows when man crowds the Holy Spirit out of the temple that rightly is His, and makes, instead, a temple to Aphrodite. I spend countless hours trying to help men and women put back together the ruin of lives they have broken by cheapening what God made holy.

God invented relaxation. Our faith contains a commandment that we bustling Americans are always anxious to forget, "Remember your day off and keep it holy." The attempt to legislate the Sabbath Day involves us in innumerable ridiculous contradictions. I do not propose that we need any more laws. I propose that Christians take seriously what God said when He established the rhythm of work and rest. But go with me some night to the greyhound track and look at the sad faces in the long line of people waiting to bet at the $2.00 window. Ask the merchants in town what happens to sale of shoes and clothing for children while the track is in operation. Or come with me to the city jail and look at the drunk-tank where men created in the image of God are thrown to dry out in a place where they probably won't hurt themselves beyond the damage they have already done by getting drunk. People need relaxation, but somehow I don't think that's what God intended. I could mention far more destructive types of amusement than gambling and drunkenness, but you know about them too.

Jesus recognized His own need for recreation. He loved hiking, mountain climbing, and fishing. Wherever He went He took the heavenly Father with Him, and that is exactly what I mean about making your body the temple of the Holy Spirit. You don't flee from daily life; you worship God where you are.

THE DAILY WALK WITH CHRIST

If the Church building is to fulfill its purpose, we must engage in endless, monotonous, routine activities with a dust-cloth and a check-book. God forbid that our activity stop there. If your body is to be the temple of the Holy Spirit, you must take care of yourself, sharing the daily humdrum with the Lord. Stopping at this point, and forgetting the neighbor whom Christ came to save, is the surest way to drive the Holy Spirit out of the temple. But I have noticed that my friends who are most conscious of Christ's presence while washing the dishes are the ones who are on tap and ready to help the neighbor when the need rises. Don't worry, as we continue thinking about the Church, we'll be thinking plenty about your neighbor. Right now we're thinking about you, worshiping God by doing your housework, or typing accurately, or behaving like a Christian on a date. Dedicating the task of the moment to Christ makes your body the temple of the Holy Spirit.

The prophet Isaiah summed together the whole mystery of daily worship in a confusing world:

> They who wait for the Lord shall renew their strength,
>   they shall mount up with wings like eagles,
>   they shall run and not be weary,
>   they shall walk and not faint.
>
>   40:31.

In our brash way, we improve upon the prophet's description. We picture ourselves walking along spiritually, and then we break into a lope. Pretty soon we spread our wings, and whoops, we are airborne.

No, the prophet had it right. Even a jet transport must come to earth. To be sure, we can send up a rocket that will circle our world indefinitely, but when we put an astronaut in it, we provide for his return. Spiritual flights come, rarely. Somewhat more frequently, we run for a while with the Lord. But most of Christian life is a walk.

The daily walk with Christ is a metaphor. The temple of the Holy Spirit is another metaphor. And the two mean exactly the same thing. Do what you must do today with Christ.

4

RESTORING THE BODY OF CHRIST
I Corinthians 3:3-11

I Corinthians 3:3-11

For while there is jealousy and strife among you, are you not of the flesh, and behaving like ordinary men? For when one says, "I belong to Paul," and another, "I belong to Apollos," are you not merely men?

What then is Apollos? What is Paul? Servants through whom you believed, as the Lord assigned to each. I planted, Apollos watered, but God gave the growth. So neither he who plants nor he who waters is anything, but only God who gives the growth. He who plants and he who waters are equal, and each shall receive his wages according to his labor. For we are fellow workmen for God; you are God's field, God's building.

According to the commission of God given to me, like a skilled master builder I laid a foundation, and another man is building upon it. Let each man take care how he builds upon it. For no other foundation can anyone lay than that which is laid, which is Jesus Christ.

4

RESTORING THE BODY OF CHRIST

I Corinthians 3:3-11

Body and flesh: the two seem almost the same, yet their meanings are almost totally different. The Church is the Body of Christ. Your body is the temple of the Holy Spirit. How could a word express more glory? "While there is jealousy and strife among you, are you not of the flesh?" Could you pack more shame into a word only five letters long? Paul was careful in his use of terms, if not always slavishly consistent. So it is no accident that two expressions, so close together, are so far apart.

THE MEANING OF FLESH

In his letter to the Galatians Paul shows what he means by flesh:

> The works of the flesh are plain: immorality, impurity, licentiousness, idolatry, sorcery, enmity, strife, jealousy, anger, selfishness, dissension, party spirit, envy, drunkenness, carousing and the like.
>
> Galatians 5:19-21.

Included in this list are some items we would never think of calling fleshly lusts: idol worship, sorcery, and party spirit do not qualify today. As I said, Paul is not slavishly consistent. Rarely he uses "body" to signify moral wrong, and frequently he uses "flesh" as a morally neutral term, meaning physical

life in the world. Living *for* the world is the evil sense which
Paul generally connotes by "flesh."

God created your body, and gave you a will to control its
tumultuous desires. When your will is in harmony with
God's will, then your body is the temple of the Holy Spirit.
But sometimes the opposite happens and your desires control
your will. This, the Apostle calls "flesh." It is fairly normal
human conduct, but Christians are called to live on a higher
level than "ordinary men." Your body means human nature
fulfilling its divine function. "Flesh" means human nature re-
sisting the upward call.

We Christians are familiar with "flesh." Our baptism does
not automatically cancel jealousy and strife. Most of us find
it hard to be consistently Christian, and so it was in ancient
Corinth. Within ourselves we fight a continuous struggle between body and flesh, or put it this way, a struggle between
what we are and what we ought to be. And perhaps this
helps to explain why a careful thinker, whose intention was to
help us in Christian living, not to confuse us further, chose
similar words to express different meanings.

The difference between your body and your flesh is clear.
The flesh is muscular and dermal tissue, while the body is
the whole mysterious complex of bone, flesh, nerve, blood and
will. The flesh is a part. The body is complete. This, I believe, is what Paul means when he expresses different thoughts
with similar words.

God made your flesh, and declared it good. But flesh isolated from the Spirit is restless, filled with seething desire, at
war with itself, incomplete. When your body is the temple of
the Holy Spirit, then you are complete, the person God created you to be. Then your flesh carries out its divinely given
function, which is not to command but to obey.

FLESH AND THE CHURCH

The Church is the Body of Christ. Its members are people,
all liberally endowed with flesh. In Corinth there was a dis-
heartening squabble among Christians. Some said, "I follow
Paul." Some said, "I follow Apollos." And those eternal irri-
tants looked benignly at both and said, "Ah, but we've got

it straight, we follow Christ." I regret that the matter has more than a historical interest. I seem to have heard twentieth century Christians disagreeing with one another. One says, "I follow Luther." Another says, "I follow Calvin." And still we have those who put us both straight saying, "But I follow Christ."

At this moment a consultation on Church union is in painfully slow progress. People with such diverse understanding of Church organization as Methodists, Presbyterians, Congregationalists, Episcopalians, Brethren, and Disciples are seriously talking about organic union. I know some Christians who say, "The thing is impossible." I do not agree with them but I can at least understand them. Then I know other Christians who have decided that Jesus was mistaken in His comment about the beam and the mote, and they oppose Church union on the ground that some Episcopalians burn incense, or Disciples have a free-wheeling concept of Church order. I readily concede that others differ, but I keep hearing our Savior's stern injunction:

> Hypocrite, first take the log out of your own eye, and then you will see clearly to take the speck out of your brother's eye.
>
> Matthew 7:5.

In current discussions about Church union the question of bishops must be discussed. Either the Church of tomorrow will have them, or it won't. (We shall need some kind of supervisory officers, and "bishop" has stronger Biblical support than "executive.") I know a Presbyterian who frequently rises to bray, and whatever the subject he is misinformed about he always mentions that at least in the Presbyterian Church we don't have bishops. He is badly mistaken. If he would re-examine his ordination vows he would discover that we follow the ancient Celtic practice, in which a "bishop" oversees a congregation rather than a diocese. Every Presbyterian minister is ordained a bishop. I recognize that comparisons are invidious, so I will limit myself to saying that when it comes to this question of bishops I have met some Episcopalians who are almost as stuffy as some Presbyterians.

At one consultation on Church union the largest monkey-wrench thrown into the gear-box was supplied by a Methodist bishop who insisted that in the Church of tomorrow bishops must have far more authority than the Episcopalians are willing to provide. Thus we have three groups of Christians: Episcopalians who want bishops to have much glory but little power, Methodists who give bishops much power but little glory, and Presbyterians who name all their ministers bishops and give us neither. Sorry material for tomorrow's Church? Without Christ our flesh is hopeless.

God's holy Word is explicit: Christ is immeasurably more important than any Church machinery. What then is Apollos? What is Paul? What is Luther? What is Arminius? What are bishops? What are presbyters? Servants through whom we believed as the Lord assigned to each.

Don't under-rate the difficulties and importance of constructing and maintaining adequate Church machinery. Thirty or forty years ago several Protestant denominations in an overseas area, that here will be nameless, decided to quit competing and to work together. The term "ecumenicity" was not in wide-spread use at the time, but the idea was well advanced. I regret that the results have not been especially inspiring.

It is difficult to drive an automobile through heavy traffic. But the difficulty is increased immeasureably if one has a rich fund of contradictory advice from the back seat:

"Turn left at this corner."

"No, turn right."

"There's a truck coming out from that side street, dear."

"STOP."

The term I used above was "work" together. Somehow when people with slightly different ways of going about the job try to cooperate they manage to get in one another's hair. In this particular area of alleged cooperation people meet frequently and disagree in a refined sort of way, and nothing much happens because there are no clearly defined lines of authority. Nobody is quite sure who is the quarterback and nobody gets his hands on the ball long enough to run with it. The net result is that the native church is still sitting on the bench instead of winning the game. So, what's the conclusion? Shall we sit back and moan because our job is difficult, or shall we get along with the task that God clearly outlines for us in the holy Bible?

The free world puts few insurmountable obstacles in the way of Church union. The obstacles are provided by flesh, which might be described as our love for Church machinery rather than the charity the machine is supposed to produce. Two Churches in a little village that I know well, one Methodist and one Presbyterian, struggled along at a half-dying rate for fifty years or so, while everyone muttered that it was a shame. Finally the two joined, and the angels prematurely applauded. The union lasted for one unhappy year, and then the two went their separate ways. The only satisfactory explanation I ever heard for this tragic divorce was, "We wanted to have a Ladies Aid just like we always had, but those people wanted a Women's Society for Christian Service." So while a group of supposed adults was squabbling about a name, nobody was aided and nobody was served, least of all the Lord.

Church organization is important. It is important that we know where we hope to go, and how we expect to get there, and who is responsible for what while we are on the way. Every other corporation must be intelligently organized to produce results; so must the Body of Christ which gave the world the idea of corporation. It is the shame of the Church that others organized around a lesser purpose than ours have solved organizational problems more successfully than we. Examine the inter-service cooperation among the armed forces, organized around the high ideal of patriotism. We notice the frequent minor flare-ups but take it for granted when soldiers, sailors and aviators with their thousand diverse skills work together to achieve the national purpose. Our country has many great corporations organized about the profit motive. The Consultation on Church Union faces no problems so difficult as those General Motors solved many years ago. On Cape Kennedy a corporation called NASA is successfully co-ordinating efforts from many different individuals and groups in order to achieve a manned flight to the moon. It is no credit to us Christians that we stand back and

glower at each other instead of out-doing these giant corporations in the thing where we are supposed to excel.

Paul asks, "While there is jealousy and strife, are you not
of the flesh and behaving like ordinary men?" In the three
instances mentioned above, ordinary men — who know all
about jealousy and strife — are out-doing the Church in organization to achieve a purpose.

Church machinery is important. Christ is more important.
Who is Paul? Who is Apollos? Who is Luther? Who is
Calvin? Or, for all that, who are Tillich and Barth? Never will
I say that these dedicated giants are nothing. Each in his
way served the Lord valiantly. Paul planted, Apollos watered,
Luther hoed, Calvin weeded, but God gives the increase.
The increase we are after is Christ-like character.

THE FRUIT OF THE FLESH

I wouldn't be saying all these nice things about the Church
if I did not love the earthly institution, the Church visible.
When I get to heaven and finally can identify the Church
invisible, or distinguish the soul from the body if you prefer,
I trust that I shall love it too. But right now all my dealings
are with the Church more-or-less Militant which, I keep
praying, may turn into the Church Triumphant. I love this
earth-bound institution. Contrary to the proverb, love makes
one more critical, not less, because one cares deeply.

The Church today is fragmented into denominations, most
of which came into being to defend some cherished belief or
practice. But time goes on, new members enter the denominations, old fires grow dim and fresh blazes spring up, and pretty
soon the new denomination looks remarkably like the old.
The cleavages between the denominations today are nowhere
near as deep as the cleavages that exist within practically
every denomination that has been here for more than a couple
of generations.

In the Book of Revelation we discover that the early Church
had weaknesses just as we do. But the Holy Spirit, working
through the imperfect organization, brought about an inward
renewal of such depth and power that the Church was able,
within a couple of centuries, to conquer the Roman Empire.

The Holy Spirit has not gone out of business. The same divine power still works the miracle of inward renewal. The old denominations are not quite so moribund as their critics always assume, not while the Holy Spirit lives. If the human effort given to dividing the Church had been used instead to strengthen and purify the existing Church, the world today would not be quite such a hell of a mess. (I am using hell accurately.)

I could list quite a few disastrous results of denominationalism in the United States today, but I will mention only one: competition among those who ought to be cooperating. Competition in business is good, most of the time. But competition in spiritual things is akin to blasphemy. I could tell a thousand stories to illustrate, but again will limit myself. A successful executive moved from Cleveland to Buffalo. A few weeks later he was back in Cleveland on a business errand, and he remarked to a friend, "Twenty-three Churches in Buffalo have approached us during the past two months, soliciting our membership. With all the heartbreaking poverty in Buffalo, that's where the Church's effort goes, competing for us rich people."

The Churches are so busy competing that we do not have time and strength for elementary charity. Most cities in the United States have Lutherans and the Assembly of God and Congregationalists and a lot of other fine people, who meet together occasionally and talk about unity of purpose, but are strangely mute about unity of action. There is none to talk about. Each congregation is busy helping needy families, on a hit-or-miss basis, but most cities lack an over-all Protestant welfare agency. We who scream loudest about the separation of Church and State have, by our failure to unite, ceded to the State our responsibility. The State, not the Church, is organized to help the helpless with their material needs, which means that the poor do not have the gospel preached to them. We produce plenty of oratory, but the poor are deaf to our words; it's only our actions they can hear, and our actions say that we do not really care enough to pool our good intentions and make them effective. Not long ago I heard about one poor family in a typical American city who achieved a squalid form of luxury by receiving substantial help from

six different congregations, while others — as everybody
knows — receive none.

There is no need to belabor the point; during the past
twenty-five years everyone with whom I have talked seriously
about the Church has mentioned the sad result of our division.
And sometimes I think the outsiders are more concerned
about it than the insiders. They look wistfully to us for help,
and find us too busy competing to care. I limit my remarks
about denominationalism because I am poking a finger into a
spot already sore. I want to heal the wound, not aggravate
it.

THE FOUNDATION

The Apostle Paul was not privileged to study English under
my teacher in High School, whom I recall as one of the
finest teachers, and finest persons, I have ever met. I can
picture her strong angular writing in the note she would have
penned if Paul had submitted this essay to her.

> Paul: Your thought is excellent, but the next time pick a
> figure of speech and stick with it. Here you are talking
> about one thing but first you call it a body, then a field, and
> then a building.

Of course, Paul was writing a letter, not a formal essay. His
imagination frequently out-stripped his pen. I am glad in
this case that he mixed his figures of speech because in doing
so he gave the answer that must guide all our discussions
about Church union.

> No other foundation can anyone lay than that which is
> laid, which is Jesus Christ.
>
> I Corinthians 3:11.

Naturally as we Christians are talking about union with
one another we must raise questions about our dealing with
others who are not Christian. Once I was talking with a
Mohammedan who said, "Why don't we all get together? If
you Protestants would give up Christ, and the Catholics would
give up the pope, we Mohammedans would give up Mecca,
and we could all be one happy family." I have long prayed

for the day when people who now are Mohammedans and those who are now Roman Catholics and those who are now Protestants will be one family, but not at the price my friend suggests. I am willing to give up a great deal of the organization to which I am accustomed. I am anxious to give up a great deal of the baptized triviality I know. But give up Christ? Long before me another troubled Christian said, "Lord, to whom shall we go? You have the words of eternal life" (John 6:68).

Try Paul's sentence again:

> No other foundation can anyone lay than that which is laid, which is the essential unity of all religions.

The idea is palatable today. It is easy to swallow and impossible to digest. The idea was wide-spread in the Roman Empire when the divine Son of God walked and talked on earth. His followers thought it grossly insufficient in those days. Passing centuries have not really improved it.

We who call ourselves Christian recognize the dignity in every man regardless of his faith or lack of it. We must live in charity toward those with whom we agree and those with whom we disagree. We must co-operate with others who hold a different faith, but in doing so we dare not sell out the belief that makes us Christian. I propose instead that we practice it — together.

Jesus Christ is here in this world today. He is the final Victor over the forces that still are crucifying Him. We who call Him Savior are His hands, His feet. If my hands and my feet weren't united any better than the Christian denominations I would be in a wheel-chair.

We are the field where Paul planted and Apollos watered, and God is trying to grow Christ-like character. It might be about time that we plants recognize our similarity rather than boasting about our difference.

We are the building. Christ is the Foundation. Paul is one master mason who cut the stones. Apollos is another who laid them firmly in place. John Wesley faithfully mixed the mortar. Alexander Campbell was a skilled tool dresser. Construction has gone on for twenty centuries until today the building stands in every nation on earth. Much of the work has been solid. Some must be torn out.

The practical conclusion of the matter is: "Let each man take care how he builds." In any other building different people contribute different skills. The banker arranges the financing. The architect draws the plan. The carpenter saws and hammers. The roofer roofs and the plumber plumbs. So in the Church different people make different contributions.

Sometimes we are more concerned about the individual contribution than our over-all purpose. Presbyterians get all excited about creeds. Episcopalians are concerned about ritual. Disciples rejoice in one type of Church organization, Methodists in an almost completely different type. Certainly I do not disparage creeds, organization, or ways of worship, but I point out that Jesus considered them secondary matters. When seekers came asking to see His credentials Jesus said,

> The blind receive their sight and the lame walk, lepers are cleansed and the deaf hear, and the dead are raised up, and the poor have good news preached to them.
>
> Matthew 11:5.

I know only one other working definition for charity that can compare with this. It was provided by the Apostle Paul in his beloved thirteenth chapter of First Corinthians, where he said that all our religious paraphernalia without charity is nothing.

I am pleading for Church unity, not because there is virtue in bigness (there is no virtue in smallness either), not because the world needs another huge power structure, but because Christ is one and we who are supposed to be His Body ought to be one, in charity. While we stand apart from one another we are "flesh." When together we express the Spirit of Christ we are His Body.

5

WORSHIP
Psalm 100

Psalm 100

Make a joyful noise unto the Lord, all ye lands.
Serve the Lord with gladness: come before his presence with
    singing.
Know ye that the Lord he is God: it is he that hath made us,
    and not we ourselves; we are his people, and the sheep of his
    pasture.
Enter into his gates with thanksgiving, and into his courts with
    praise: be thankful unto him, and bless his name.
For the Lord is good; his mercy is everlasting; and his truth
    endureth to all generations.

Authorized Version

5

WORSHIP

Psalm 100

The one hundredth psalm calls for the whole earth to join in worship: Red China, Cuba, the United Arab Republic, you, me, everybody. This is a short psalm, only five verses, 86 words in English (40 in Hebrew). Its pattern is clear. The first verse is the call to worship. The second and fourth verses telling why we worship are dovetailed into the third and fifth which suggest how to worship.

THE CALL TO WORSHIP

The psalm is one of many places where the Holy Bible claims that worship is man's chief business in life. Other matters are important; worship is most important. Since this is the exact opposite of modern man's thought about the matter, we should re-examine what we mean by worship.

Worship is a human activity in which we seek an encounter with the divine. It is what we do to recognize and respond to the fact that "the Lord, he is God." It includes what we do in Church, and it ought to include what we do all week when we are not in Church. Another psalm, underscoring the seven-day aspect of worship says, "His praise shall continually be in my mouth." If you seriously try to go through life with an unending mutter of praise on your lips, you will neither worship nor accomplish anything else, and strangers will look at you in a worried manner. The words without concentration are empty. If you try to concentrate on words of praise while you are driving a nail, for instance, you will bash your thumb and mar the woodwork, and your thoughts will not be worshipful. The verbal flow is not what the Lord wants, but the dedicated heart. Learn to make each hammer stroke an act of prayer by dedicating your whole life to Christ. The hour of worship in the Lord's house on the Lord's day is one of God's greatest helps toward a totally dedicated life.

I said that the psalm is about worship, and nobody batted an eye, although the word "worship" does not occur in it. Instead we find another term "serve" that means today what worship ought to mean. "Serve" in modern English means both what we do in Church and the ways we express our faith in the community. Unhappily, we have narrowed "worship" to mean only the sort of thing we do in Church: prayer, hymns, sacrament, meditation, Scripture, and the self-dedication that is symbolized when we offer our tithes. We call what we are doing right now either "morning worship" or "Church service" with no difference in meaning. Sometimes we call it "worship-service" which is just as bad as saying "worship-worship" or "service-service."

Our dividing worship and service has led some to misunderstand Jesus when He says, "You cannot serve God and mammon." Actually, I have heard people say this means that a Christian cannot receive a pay-check or sell goods at a reasonable profit. But substitute identical words, and you have a perfectly reasonable and totally undeniable statement: "You cannot worship God and money." Most of you, engaged in one kind of business or another, serve God while faithfully doing your daily work. God's children depend on each other. We could not live without the farmer, the truck-driver, and the grocer. If they are working to help their neighbors, they serve God on the job. If they are working solely for the pay-check, they serve mammon.

Not long ago I encountered crude mammon-worship in our neighborhood. A young man from another city was employed by a firm here. During their first interview his new boss said, "You'll want a nice respectable car. Nothing flashy, you understand, but nice. And you'll want a nice, respectable house. Nothing flashy, you know, but nice. And you'll want to join a nice, respectable Church. I'd suggest that you try being a Presbyterian. We don't have any Presbyterians on our staff now, and you'll meet a nice class of people there."

The young man came to me, so angry he could hardly sputter. I gather that I was the first clergyman he had ever talked with. And he seemed surprised to discover that I was just as angry as he was, though for a different reason. He thought his private life his own business (and I concur), but I was angry because someone was trying to use God as a profit-making gimmick. We do have a nice class of people in the Church — Jesus called them the salt of the earth — but they don't worship each other. They worship God.

The young man and I are good friends today. He still has his job. Perhaps as a result of our conversation he is reading Christian literature for the first time in his life. He knows that he is welcome to visit our Church any time, and that we want him as a member, just as soon as his intention is to worship God. Sometimes I think he is coming our way, sometimes not. But he has firmly grasped at least one Christian principle. Worship is directed to God; it is not the means to any earthly goal.

The hundredth psalm is about the part of worship that takes place in the Church building:

> Enter into His gates with thanksgiving and into His courts with praise.

The psalm invites a person's bodily presence in a material structure. The Temple gates were heavy wooden doors in a gigantic stone gateway that led through a massive wall into the court, an area several acres in extent surrounding the Holy Temple and the high altar. This Church building means somewhat the same thing to you and me that the Temple meant to the psalmist. Our service resembles that in Jerusalem, when people gathered in a sacred place at scheduled hours to sing and pray their thanksgiving to the Lord. And that is the part of worship I am talking about, though we all recognize that balancing the books or rocking a cradle are likewise acts of worship.

Worship is the Church activity that most annoys modern

man. When he looks seriously at our program, he applauds, until he looks seriously at the reason for the program.

Once in the tropics I was visiting a mission station with a friend who is not a Christian. I have rarely seen anyone quite so excited as he was about the little schoolhouse and the hospital. He said, "This I can understand. Here you are helping people." Then, with a slight gesture of distaste, he pointed to the Chapel, and he said, "But why do you have to drag in all this religion?" I said first, that our love for teaching and medicine did not bring us to that hostile clime; our love for the heavenly Father brought us there and required us to bring along the best our civilization has to offer. I added that the way has been wide open several centuries, and for some strange reason, people like him who enthuse over humanity and restrain their enthusiasm about the divine have not cared enough for other people to dig into their pockets and support mission schools and hospitals, until, in the quite recent past, governments have undertaken international welfare work. When governments hostile to ours do it, we always can discern a tinge of self-interest.

The Church learned to care about people because we worship our heavenly Father, who tells us with His ever firm love that outward worship is hypocrisy if we are not striving to meet human need.

Human need is always visible. God is invisible. Hence many have decided to concentrate on the visible and forget the divine. Somehow, though, people who turn aside from worship sooner or later find themselves turning back. If a man does not worship God, he will erect god-substitutes and worship them.

About the time the psalm was written (give or take a few centuries) two great philosophers, Confucius and Gautama Buddha, attempted to eliminate worship from human life. Both said that the Prime Cause is unknowable; people should not waste time and strength seeking to know what is beyond their reach. Obviously, it is futile to pray to we-know-not-what; so as a substitute for prayer and similar acts of worship, they taught their followers to meditate about virtue and duty. Both outlined a noble course of action, most of which a Christian can applaud. But something happened among those who followed both these great thinkers: people came to worship the teacher who had decried worship. Today many pray to Confucius and Buddha, who taught them not to pray.

Karl Marx said that religion is the opium of the people, an exercise in fantasy that keeps us from putting our thought and effort where they can do the most good. The Communists say that worship distracts attention from man's important business — production — and sure enough, while we are in Church we are not producing any cement blocks. Then they set up their own worship-apparatus, complete with sacred dogma, holy days, saints, martyrs, and pilgrimages to hallowed shrines. They demand an allegiance to the Party that a Christian will allow only to God. And they put on magnificent demonstrations, pageants, and parades, all designed to focus attention and devotion on what they believe is central, which is similar to our purpose in public worship and much more time consuming.

Worship is an indispensible part of life. Take away true worship, false will rush in. When the psalm calls all the lands to worship the Lord, it means that we who know Him in Jesus Christ are obliged to share what we know with those whose knowledge is twisted or incomplete. Neither here nor anywhere else does the Holy Bible agree with the genial mish-mash of contemporary thought that it doesn't matter to whom you pray: Buddha, Confucius, a little stone tiki, Shiva, Stalin, or, if your thoughts happen to run in that direction, God. We who know God as revealed in Jesus Christ are called to live and work so that others may know the heavenly Father through us, else our worship is blasphemous noise.

WHY DO WE WORSHIP

If all of life is — or ought to be — worship, why take part of life to enter a hallowed place for worship? Common sense, the psalms, our neighbor who worships mammon, and the Lord Jesus Christ all agree that coming here is no guarantee of worship when we get here. We may actually let it keep us from worship, by spreading a pious smokescreen between ourselves and God. It is possible to abuse any good thing.

Is this thing we are talking about — worship — really good? Do we need times set apart for worship in a place dedicated to that purpose? The psalmist evidently thought that we do when he said, "Enter into His gates."

In every other department of life we must concentrate on one thing at a time. Many of you know far more about house-keeping than I will ever know. How do you go about it? Sometimes you wash dishes, sometimes you dust furniture, sometimes you make beds, sometimes you water the plants, and sometimes you make plans, yet all the time you are keeping house. The time spent making plans is perhaps the most important single item on the list. Without a plan, you can toil mightily and accomplish nothing. Worship is something like that. What we do here is, in part, planning how to worship on Tuesday and Wednesday.

It is easy and natural for us to be distracted in public worship. Daily cares and responsibilities crowd our minds. The woman three rows ahead is wearing a garish hat that makes it hard for us to think deeply about God, and those noisy children are acting even worse than usual. Distraction is easy; it always has been. But staying away from the Church building does not eliminate distraction.

Worship and practically everything else needs the self-reinforcing action that we call habit. If you come intending to worship, and succeed in doing so, the next time you come your physical surroundings will help suggest Him who is eternal and invisible. If you want to do anything successfully — banking, baking, or barbering — you need good working habits, and these usually include a working place. In our constantly distracting world, Christian experience has demonstrated for two thousand years that those who habitually worship God in the Church on the Lord's day are more likely to worship Him on Thursday than their neighbors whose approach to the divine is casual and sporadic.

The focus in worship is never upon ourselves and our psychological needs, however important these may be, but on God. The psalm suggests three basic ideas about God that ought frequently to run through our minds while we are in His house, and all the rest of the time:

> Know ye that the Lord He is God.
> It is He that hath made us and not we ourselves.
> We are His people and the sheep of His pasture.

The first thought appears obvious. "The Lord He is God." Is it really so obvious, when you consider the number who deny it, either in word or in act?

Many scholars believe that an unknown poet wrote the psalm while the Hebrew people were in Babylon, where their neighbors believed that Marduk was God. This is not merely another label for the same reality. The Babylonians worshiped the forces of nature and called them Marduk. Their faith contained some truth and much error. Rephrase what the psalmist says, "Know that the Lord [not nature] is God."

Today, without being quite so honest about it as the Babylonians, people elevate other forces and powers to the first place in life: wealth, pleasure, and power, chief among them. These all are good; we have no quarrel with any of them, but none of them is God. In worship we recognize Him who is almighty, in whose service is the fullest joy, from whom comes all our riches, material and spiritual.

> Know ye that the Lord He is God.
> It is He that hath made us and not we ourselves.

God created everything that Marduk represented. When we look at the world situation and decide (correctly) that it is a mess, we ought to recall that the mess is a human construction built upon the divine order. The beauty of the earth and the glory of the sky, with the incredible miracle of life, all came into being without any good advice from us. This gives reason to believe that He who made the majestic mountains and the delicate flowers will complete His creation. His Kingdom will come on earth.

When the world was ready, God created man. It is no shame to be a creature. The trouble starts when we creatures confuse ourselves with the Creator. Two people once said, "If we just defy the Lord in this small matter, then we shall be as gods." And the world has been a mess ever since. If you want to know where you are going, it helps to know

where you have come from. At worship we look to our
divine Source.

> Know ye that the Lord He is God.
> It is He that hath made us and not we ourselves.
> We are His people and the sheep of His pasture.

"We are His people" may be the most frequently misunder-
stood thought in the Bible. We are God's people, chosen,
elect, pre-destined. Those who believe themselves divinely
chosen have sometimes acted as if this were, in effect, getting
a lollipop for being such a bright boy. God's chosen people
— I am referring to Christian people — have occasionally been
smug about the choice.

Why did God choose you? Most of us will admit, without
much arguing, that others are prettier and wealthier and
more educated, or possibly they can hit a baseball farther than
we can. He did not choose us because we are so outstand-
ing. He chose us to serve Him.

It is no real flattery to be called a sheep — as many psalms
call us. A farmer raises sheep to serve him. God has chosen
us to serve Him. This is what election means: not privilege
— duty; not prestige — work. When I look at all the mis-
directed energy in the world today, I can but echo the Psalm:
know that the Lord has chosen you to do His work.

Why do we worship? Because the Lord is God. Because
He made us. Because He chose us. And — developing the
thought, "the Lord He is God," — because:

> The Lord is good,
> His mercy is everlasting,
> And His truth endureth to all generations.

Three words stand out: "good," "mercy," "truth." And a fourth,
"everlasting," binds them together. The psalmist knew, just
as we do, that the world is constantly changing. Mountains
erode into hillocks, and new islands are born beneath the
ocean. But we think so much about the change that we have
almost forgotten the unchanging, and we express our mental
poverty by abusing a respectable scientific term "relativity,"
which Dr. Einstein used to describe what light does in inter-

galactic space and similar matters that you and I don't know much about.

Things are changing, and different people have different customs, true. But a few realities are here to stay. Three plus two equals five was true yesterday and will be true tomorrow. We may express the truth with different languages or different numerical systems, but the thing expressed remains. Goodness, mercy, and truth likewise endure to all generations. They are relative, if you wish, to God's eternity.

It is easy to forget goodness, mercy, and truth in our frequently cruel generation. Recently a vocal Presbyterian took me apart because our Church has urged that we try to keep open the channels of communication with the Communists, against whom we are at war. He said, "This is appeasement. [It isn't.] Doesn't the Church know these people are cruel and heartless liars?" Yes the Church knows it only too well. Our Church was warning people about Communism when they thought it an interesting agricultural reform. I think my friend was urging that we try to be more false, cruel, and heartless than the Communists. If that is our strategy, we are whipped. We have our standing orders, "Be not overcome with evil, but overcome evil with good." Goodness is everlasting, not evil. Mercy will triumph, not cruelty. Falsehoods will come and go, but truth endures to all generations. We worship God because He and He alone is eternal. We worship Him by doing what is fit to endure.

Probably the unknown poet in Babylon composed the hundredth psalm when it was beginning to seem possible that the Hebrew exiles might return to Jerusalem. We yawn while we read the ancient history: The Babylonian Empire rotted at the heart, and Cyrus the Persian was able to overthrow it. When he came to power, he allowed the exiles to return. But what is dull history to us, twenty-five centuries later, was filled with confusion and terror for the people who lived through it. They hated the present and dreaded the future, with its all-embracing uncertainty and constant danger. In time of national upheaval nothing seems fixed, everything is chaos. But God is eternal.

Twenty-five centuries have elapsed since the psalm was composed, seventy-five generations of experience to show whether or not the psalmist speaks truth when he says "everlasting." What, beside our faith, has endured from ancient Babylon? Archaeologists have discovered the ruins of magnificent palaces and libraries. They can trace the once stately walls that surrounded the great city, and they have mapped in the desert an irrigation system that modern engineers could well be proud of. Ruins: stately, majestic, crumbling ruins. Nothing else endures from ancient Babylon but the faith that grew and developed among a people who hated the place.

Why do we worship God?

> Because the Lord is good,
> His mercy is everlasting,
> And His truth endureth to all generations.

Twenty-five centuries from now, if the human race has not yet finished its course, Dr. Einstein's work may well seem crude and primitive, and perhaps archaeologists will proudly exhibit the ruins that were New York, but people will be worshiping the divine love that endures to all generations.

HOW DO WE WORSHIP?

The hundredth, like most of the other psalms, is suggestive rather than exhaustive. It has not listed all the reasons why we worship, nor does it tell in detail how to worship. If you would know how the Hebrews worshiped in olden times, you should read the Book of Leviticus, where you will find more detail than your mind can assimilate about their elaborate ceremony and ritual. And the ancient Hebrews, I feel quite safe in saying, would find it bewildering if they could be here with us now. But one or two things mentioned in the psalm remain crystal clear and understandable across the generations:

> Enter into His gates with thanksgiving and into His courts with praise.

The psalmist is talking about people who assemble in a dedicated place to worship God. If the scholars are right, that he wrote the psalm when exiled from Jerusalem, his words become poignant and all the more forceful.

The exile showed, among other things, that faith in God can survive when the Temple is destroyed and the city walls of Jerusalem are torn down. And as soon as it was humanly possible for the exiles to return, what did they do? They restored the walls and rebuilt the Temple. Why? God is everywhere, but you must be somewhere. You need to concentrate. The biggest possible help to concentration upon God is public worship: entering a place dedicated to God, joining others who have come there to worship Him, and uniting your voice with their voices in praise and thanks.

The ancient Hebrews sang. As I meet with Protestants here and there about the United States, I am deeply concerned about the quality of worship reflected in dull, lackluster singing. Last summer I spent two happy months ministering to a Church in Scotland. I suppose fifty people in the States, after discussing the heather, have asked how public worship in Scotland compares with ours. I have told all fifty that most differences are trivial, and not all of them favor Scotland. But one contrast shines out. My Scottish friends sing from the heart, my friends in the United States mumble piously. Hearing this, American Christians usually say, "Oh, I suppose the Scots have better voices." And I answer, "No, they don't. They use their voices better."

> Make a joyful noise unto the Lord, all ye lands,
> Serve the Lord with gladness,
> Come before His presence with singing.

Why do we sing at worship? For one thing, when faith is strong, people cannot help singing. We Christians have something to be joyful about. Strong, joyous faith almost always bursts into song. The great ages of faith have, without exception, produced great church music.

Curiously, music has another function that seems to be the exact opposite: it strengthens a weak faith. Song reaches into dark and dismal places, where reason and logic are forbidden to enter. Where was our country's greatest music produced? In the elegant salons of colonial Philadelphia or Boston? You know it was not. In the music departments of our universities? Scarcely. Our great music came from the slave cabins.

I had an upsetting experience several years ago that illustrates how music can bring light to dark places. One Sunday I noticed a stranger in Church, sitting directly in front of a family who love to sing. They are not soloists, but they sing: mother, father, a boy whose voice had just changed, a girl about twelve or so, and a couple of little children. After Church the stranger shook my hand at the door and said, "I was planning to kill myself after Church this morning, but the way you people sang made me change my mind. Good day, sir." I have never seen him since. And I will raise a question that you, better than anyone else, can answer. Had you been sitting behind him that Sunday would he have carried through with his original plan?

In imagination visit the ancient Hebrew Temple as our fathers are gathering together for a holy day. You can understand why they are assembling; you can understand why they are singing. But you must stretch your imagination to understand why they express thanks as they do. Expressing your own thanks, however, is more important than understanding theirs.

At the center of the Temple stood a high altar, on which the priests offered a sacrifice to express thanks, praise, and dedication, to confess sin, and to enact visibly God's invisible forgiveness. In our Church we have a table where we gather for dinner with our older Brother. We recognize the differences between ancient sacrifice and Holy Communion today; we ought likewise to see the resemblance. Worship is what we do to recognize and respond to the fact that "the Lord, He is God." Our fathers enacted this faith in a good way, we in a far better way; the difference between the two ways is Christ. During Holy Communion Protestants today usually focus their attention upon the Cross. The early Christians emphasized instead the Resurrection, and called their sacramental meal the Eucharist, or Thanksgiving. The psalm lays the stress upon thanks as the chief part of worship, which might be a remarkably good example for us to follow.

We in the United States have more blessings — materially — to be grateful for than almost any other people anywhere.

Yet if you listen, you hear us moaning the blues almost incessantly. Perhaps if we would really sing our thanksgiving hymns on Sunday, actually vibrating our vocal cords, the thought might penetrate our minds, and we might live our thanks on Wednesday. Those who spend time and energy in worship find the world a far more habitable place than their neighbors who are concerned primarily about things.

I read a fascinating magazine article recently about a family budget. The writer pictures a family, struggling along with twenty thousand a year, and going into debt all the time. He raps them lightly over the wrist and shows them how intelligent management could settle their problem.

First — in some circles, it's always mentioned first — taxes. A family must eat; so the writer provides liberally for groceries. He includes what I thought a sizeable amount for the family's liquid consumption. Keeping a roof overhead is expensive; so is driving an automobile. These matters are effectively taken care of. Naturally people must save for the children's education. Insurance, clothing, all these necessary matters are discussed in detail. When it came to recreation it seemed to me that the writer goes overboard. Since I have never shouldered the burden of spending twenty thousand dollars a year, perhaps I do not understand the strain it imposes, and the necessity for expensive relaxation. All the figures given add up exactly to twenty thousand dollars. The writer dusts his hands proudly and says, "Well, that's that. You see, by applying your intelligence to a problem, you can solve it." Perhaps you have noticed a curious omission. Not one cent, not one single solitary red copper penny, is budgeted for God.

I talk with such people all the time. I hear their querulous wail, "Why should I support the loafers? Let them work. Let the government be Santa Claus. I have to buy a new outboard motor." These people are prosperous, healthy, well fed, beautifully clothed, highly educated, and damned. What they ask from life is more. The more they receive materially, the greater becomes their spiritual poverty. If gratitude to God for lavish abundance is in their hearts, they do not mention it to me; they are too busy telling me what the government takes away. I can grow eloquent about this subject too, but I keep recalling that after the government has taken its bite we in the United States have far more material goods than almost any other people in the world.

We ought to thank God for our material blessings. We ask Him for daily bread; we ought to thank Him when we receive it. After all, you and I did not create the miracle of fertility by which a grain of wheat produces the grain that becomes bread; nor did we ordain that seedtime and harvest shall arrive on schedule. Even so, when we thank God for material blessings, we must always recognize that they can be taken away. The rich blessings of human love and friendship likewise can be lost. But there is one blessing, for which we can ever be grateful, that never can be removed: God Himself. During the exile the Hebrew people lost most of the material blessings they had known. They had all the crutches taken away from their faith, and they turned to God for strength. The psalm — if we are right about its date — is one evidence that they were grateful because God made them strong.

It is an invaluable help, when you are feeling sorry for yourself, to remember what you have to be grateful for, and I don't know a better place to do it than your Church. People are mean and rude. Yes, many are. But look around you at all the kind, warmhearted, friendly Christian people worshiping with you, and thank God for them. Our country is filled with unrest. Quite so. Would you care to move to Leningrad? Our government is so designed that you can help correct our troubles. Did you ever thank God for this responsibility? And while we are talking about blessings, have you thanked your Creator recently because Christ is risen and finally will triumph?

I do not propose that if we blissfully ignore our troubles they will disappear under the carpet. I propose that in a troubled world we praise God with our lips and with our lives for His blessings, and the supreme blessing is, "the Lord, He is God." That's what the hundredth psalm is about: your worshiping God in His house; so that you can worship Him with all the rest of your life; so that through you others will come to worship Him, until finally the whole earth is united in a joyful thanksgiving hymn to the Lord.

6

CHRISTIAN LEADERSHIP
Matthew 20:20-28

Matthew 20:20-28

Then the mother of the sons of Zebedee came up to him, with her sons, and kneeling before him she asked him for something. And he said to her, "What do you want?" She said to him, "Command that these two sons of mine may sit, one at your right hand and one at your left, in your kingdom." But Jesus answered, "You do not know what you are asking. Are you able to drink the cup that I am to drink?" They said to him, "We are able." He said to them, "You will drink my cup, but to sit at my right hand and at my left is not mine to grant, but it is for those for whom it has been prepared by my Father." And when the ten heard it, they were indignant at the two brothers. But Jesus called them to him and said, "You know that the rulers of the Gentiles lord it over them, and their great men exercise authority over them. It shall not be so among you; but whoever would be great among you must be your servant, and whoever would be first among you must be your slave; even as the Son of man came not to be served but to serve, and to give his life as a ransom for many."

6

CHRISTIAN LEADERSHIP
Matthew 20:20-28

It's easy enough to understand why the mother of James and John came to Jesus asking that her sons be the chief among His followers. She had loved these lads before they were born, and she wanted them to be leaders. They had chosen a strange career, following a most unusual person. Never mind, it was their choice, and she wanted them to have the best of it. It's easy to understand the request, and easy to understand Jesus' answer to it. But it's hard to live with the answer.

THE SPIRIT AND THE INSTITUTION

The request, which James and John presumably urged their mother to make on their behalf, showed that two men had not yet caught the spirit of Jesus' teaching. The other ten disciples were angry because James and John acted like normal human beings. Their anger shows that the ten had not yet caught the spirit of Jesus' teaching either. And to these men Jesus entrusted the task of building an institution to express the spirit that guided His life.

Wherever you find people banded together to do something, you find conflict between the spirit of what they are doing and the institution through which they do it. A general comes to treat his regiment as a problem in administration and not as a weapon. Business executives make long speeches about enterprise, responsibility, and initiative, then demonstrate in their hiring policies that these are not the qualities they want in their employees. A century ago people in the United States thought something had been accomplished when people in another land adopted a constitution and a parliamentary form of government. Today we are a little wiser, or perhaps more cynical, about the value of exporting democratic forms without exporting the democratic spirit.

The spirit restlessly probes the future. The institution of any spirit tenaciously clings to the past. A spirit is formless, an institution comes to love the forms more than the thing the forms once contained.

Jesus entrusted to twelve men the task of building an institution that would express His spirit to future ages. He knew the danger in what He was doing. The flaming spirit that led Abraham and Moses and Isaiah had been almost stifled by the crushing mass of legal observance that some Hebrews wished to substitute for spiritual life. Jesus called His people back to first principles, and He founded an institution to keep us there, knowing that an institution is in constant danger of forgetting what it is instituted to achieve.

The conflict between spirit and institution is nothing unique to the Church. But it's the Church we're thinking about, and it's the Church where we must examine the conflict. Our Savior tells us how to resolve the conflict: "Whoever would be great among you must be your servant." This is the principle of Christian leadership that must suffuse the entire earthly institution, the Church. We Christians have a message to give the world, which certainly needs to learn how to institutionalize the spirit of education, business, and government — to name only a few. We could best convey the message to the world by setting an example, rather than by giving sage advice that we fail to heed ourselves.

THE NEED FOR LEADERSHIP

Neither here nor anywhere else does Jesus deny the need for leadership in His Church. If you want to get anything done in the world, you must organize to do it. That's what we mean by institution. You need some agreed-upon ways and means of deciding what to do, and that requires leadership. In the pure democracy of a town meeting, someone must stand up in front and be chairman. Among the most primitive tribes, someone is chief. You would not ride a ship if you suspected any confusion about who is captain. When I was eight years old I overheard a conversation: to one of my colleagues his Mamma said, "Do this," and his Daddy said, "No, do the exact opposite." And I decided at the time that, maltreated as I was, still my parents had enough consideration for me to settle their disagreements in my absence. Home, shop, office, farm, city, state, nation — you name it — if it's an assembly of people, it needs leadership. The Church is no exception. Leadership is not tyranny; leadership means two or more people getting things done in an orderly way.

The Lord Jesus criticized religious leaders. In His day they were called priests, Levites, Pharisees, Sadducees, scribes, lawyers, and rabbis. The differences among these people don't concern us now, only their resemblance to ourselves. When Jesus spoke sharply to or about them, He was not attacking leadership. Quite the contrary. Our Lord spent most of His public ministry preparing leaders for His Church. He left us a battle to win, something involving the gates of hell, which will not do much crumbling without a strong attack, skillfully led.

THE MOTIVE THAT LEADS US TO SEEK LEADERSHIP

No, it isn't leadership that Jesus warns us against, but the motive that leads men to seek leadership, and the subtle corrosion it can inflict upon human character. What James and John wanted was to feel important, not to be important. Jesus asked them, "Are you able to drink the cup that I am to drink?" With the valor of ignorance, they said, "We are able." Not long after, our Lord knelt in Gethsemane and prayed, "Let this cup pass from me." Almost certainly the "cup" means the same on both occasions. It was much more than the physical pain of crucifixion. It was the spiritual pain of rejection, denial, and betrayal, that led Jesus finally to the abyss where He thought the heavenly Father had deserted

Him. "He was bruised for our iniquities." That's the cup
we're talking about: living and when needful, suffering for
others. And you can't begin to understand it until you have
suffered for the wrong someone else did, and continued loving
the person who did the wrong.

"Are you able to drink the cup that I am to drink?" They
said brashly, "We are able." And Christ made them able, not
in a day, or a week, or a year, but Christ made them able.
Christ chose two bumptious, over-confident young men as
leaders in the institutional Church. And His Spirit, working
through the Church, gradually transformed these leaders into
Christ-like men. That's what Jesus promised, that's what He
delivered — not authority for its own sake, but Christ-like
character, for God's sake.

Leadership is dangerous, but necessary, stuff. Without it you
could have no government, no industry, no school system, no
Church. We see the abuses clearly in government, where a
Stalin or a Hitler can lead a great nation to disaster. We
ought to be able to see them clearly in the Church; Jesus
talked enough about them. He pointed with devastating accuracy to the sins of religious people: Pharisees, scribes, Sadducees and rabbis. If we want to understand what He says,
we might well scratch out the ancient names and write in
Presbyterians, Fundamentalists, Evangelicals, Baptists and
Sunday School teachers. If none of these words apply to
you, put in one that does apply, and see if what Jesus says
about the ancient Pharisees sounds uncomfortable. If you
fail to bring the Bible up to date in this manner, you are
abusing God's holy Word, which is always more comfortable
than hearing Him.

The twenty-third chapter of the Gospel according to St.
Matthew is a probing analysis of the religious leader's temptations. In brief summary: We preach, but do not practice.
We lay heavy burdens on men, but will not lift a finger to
help lift these burdens. We love the ornate accouterments of
office. We love to sit at the head table, and to be greeted
in public by all the big-shots in town. We love our impres-
sive titles. We make faith so complicated that a person doesn't
know what we are talking about. We find easy evasions
for the most obvious demands of Christ. We make a holy

show of trivialities while neglecting justice, mercy, and faith. We worry about appearances, never mind the reality behind the appearance. We venerate Christ, as long as He stays decently out of contact with today, while we passionately ignore the sort of thing Christ is concerned about.

In the twenty-third chapter of Matthew's Gospel, I find the temptations I live with because I am an officer in the Christian Church. I do not suggsst that the Church should get rid of the temptation by abolishing all officers. I ask instead that we who are tempted recognize the fact, and keep our motives under constant scrutiny. The key sentence in the whole chapter is, "They do all their deeds to be seen by man."

Since people are looking at us Church officers most of the time, we ought to be conscious of the public stare and act accordingly. A Christian certainly ought to consider what his neighbor thinks about him. A Christian ought jealously to guard his reputation for integrity. A Christian ought to strive unendingly to be a person whose opinion others will hear with respect. Why? A Christian tries to be a Christ-like person, not because people are looking, but because that's what it means to be a Christian.

We aren't here to put on a holy show, we're here to serve God, and we best serve God by serving people. In Matthew 23, where Jesus examines our temptations, He repeats the self-same thought He expressed to the twelve after the squabble about James and John: "He who is greatest among you shall be your servant." This ought to be the guiding principle in all Christian leadership.

LEADERSHIP IN THE LOCAL CHURCH

Jethro, the father-in-law of Moses, gave some wise advice about Church leadership. He saw Moses smothered beneath a mountain of administrative and judicial duties, and he said, "You will wear yourself out; the thing is too heavy for you; you are not able to perform it alone." (See Exodus 18:13-23.) Then he divided the leader's work into halves: first the responsibility that can never be transferred, second the authority that can be delegated. "You shall represent the

people before God . . . and make them know the way in
which they must walk. . . ." No one can pass on to another
the responsibility of prayer and example. But Jethro continued with the delegation of authority, "Choose able men
from all the people, such as fear God, men who are trust-
worthy and who hate a bribe. . . ." These able people
received authority to help Moses carry the load. With many
leaders instead of one leader, the Children of Israel continued
to travel together, because they all followed the pillar of
cloud and the pillar of fire.

Most Protestant congregations, following Jethro's advice,
offer a bewildering variety of opportunities to exercise Christian leadership, or conversely, a bewildering variety of temptations to do the right thing for the wrong reason.

Once I was called to install the officers of our Women's Association. The secretary read out the names of the officers-
elect: President, Vice-President, Secretary, Treasurer, then
the leaders for each of eight circles. Then the various committee chairmen: Overseas Sewing, Mission Education, Church
and Society, Christian Literature, and lots more. As the list
went on and on, and each officer-elect came forward, it
struck me that the membership of the Association was dwindling rapidly, but I persevered. With the dedicatory service I
asked the leaders if they would assume their duties; then
I asked the members of the Association to signify their ac-
ceptance of the officers by rising for the dedicatory prayer.
And they both stood up.

We do not have a surplus of chiefs without enough Indians.
Our Church members are interested in many kinds of activities. We learned long ago that we can be most effective by
delegating specific authority to people who have specific abili-
ties, so that one can work out the details of our work with
retarded children while another is arranging the Bible study
class for Monday evening.

Our congregation has a nominating committee, which examines carefully the needs of the Church and the qualifica-
tions of individual members to meet these needs. And we
haven't greatly improved upon Jethro's job-description for
Church office.

After the committee has met, it is my privilege to go to

various strong men and women, who have been greatly honored in being deemed fit for heavy responsibility. It has
reached the place where I am surprised if the conversation
varies much from this pattern:

Pastor: Will you serve if elected?

Officer Candidate: I'm not good enough.

Pastor: Knowing that is the first requirement for the job.

These people are not being coy. They know me — and the
Lord — well enough not to bother about that. It's a simple
statement of fact. I'm not good enough. They know Christ
well enough to realize that they have only sipped the cup,
they haven't swallowed it. They aren't Christ-like persons,
not yet. I point out that they are heading in the right direction, as estimated by the nominating committee, and that no
one in the Church — especially the Pastor — is good enough to
represent Christ. We have this treasure in earthen vessels (II
Corinthians 4:7). The first requirement for a Church officer
is his concern for the treasure and not for the vessel that
holds it. This was what James and John flubbed.

On one occasion (in a Church far from here) the nominating committee made what I considered an unwise selection: a
big, imposing man, with great dignity, courtly manners and
loudly impeccable doctrine. Since the committee had chosen,
and since the man was eligible to serve, I believed it my duty
to approach him. He looked me square in the eye and said,
"I wondered how long it would be before you asked me, after
all I've done for the Church." He was the least valuable
Church officer I ever knew. To him Church service was a
means to public recognition. That is the exact opposite of
Jesus' standard: service is the thing that counts; public recognition is a danger that frequently goes with it.

COMING TO A DECISION IN THE LOCAL CHURCH

A management expert would pine away and die if he had
the Pastor's task of dealing with a congregation. He would
gasp weakly that the endless series of committee meetings is
not efficient. To this the only possible retort is a question:
"Efficient enough to do what?" If we are out to be empire
builders, I'll concede the point. If we are out to crumple

the gates of hell, the structure of a Protestant Church, where
many share the burdens and temptations of leadership, offers
a wonderful opportunity to do it right, coupled with the cor-
responding temptation to bungle the job. If we are genuinely
the Church, we are not concerned primarily about buildings
and budgets; we are concerned about people, both those who
aren't Church members and those who are.

Jesus told us Church officers and members, "Let your
light so shine before men that they may see your good works
and give glory to your Father who is in heaven." These are
our tactical orders for batting in the gates of hell. We're
supposed to be active in such a way that our neighbors
will come to know God through our actions. Sometimes it
doesn't work. I have met persons who were attracted to
Christianity and who entered deeply enough into Protestant
Church life to discover the nagging, back-biting pettiness
that can sometimes grieve the Holy Spirit. They decided,
"If that's what Protestantism means, I don't want any." Some
have looked to other worshiping groups; most have joined the
outsiders. Church members, by disobeying Christ, made the
Church an obstacle to Christ rather than His agent in the
world.

There are no problems in Church government, or anywhere else, as long as people agree about what they are doing
and the best way to do it. When we disagree the problems
may become acute. If a sociologist were to study the power
structure in your congregation, what would he find? I have
read a few such studies about flesh-and-blood congregations,
and sometimes it seems that Jesus never admonished His
Church about dangers inherent in all leadership. Most of the
studies, happily, show people trying to exercise good humor
and common courtesy in reaching decisions. Church organization can either deny or express Christ.

In the world where men of good will disagree, still we must
decide what the group is to do, and reaching this decision is
the place where Christ's leadership standard must be exer-
cised. If two people disagree about a matter of fact, they
can both be wrong; it is not logically possible that both
are completely right. Usually the situation is one where there
is much to be said on both sides of the question. But in this

ambiguous world we must decide, upon the half-knowledge that is ours.

Let's imagine a situation in the local Church where you and your neighbor disagree, and the Church must act. And let's agree in advance that you are right and the other fellow is wrong. What's to do?

Once two Christians disagreed about something important, and one of them said, "Let's pray about this." The other answered, "I'll pray for you, but I will not pray with you." I have never seen blasphemy against the Holy Ghost satisfactorily defined, but I consider this a pretty good specimen. We who are Christian are supposed to use our disagreements to strengthen the bonds of love, not to sever them. And the Lord never promised that it would be easy.

What's to do? Perhaps the first thing to do is to re-examine your own idea, and make completely sure that you're holding it because it's right, and not because it's yours. It's painful to give up a cherished idea. But isn't that part of the cup which Jesus asks his disciples to drink?

What's to do? The next step, after you have examined the idea in private, preferably on your knees, is to present it to the responsible group within the Church. There you advance your idea with all the vigor at your disposal. You bring out arguments in its favor and you refute the arguments against it. This part is relatively easy. Then comes the hard part. You sit and listen while the other person is arguing against your idea and refuting the truth you have so eloquently spoken. You slam back at the other person's arguments with all your strength and skill. But here's the difference that Jesus Christ wants to make: the other person is sacred; you do not attack his motives, you do not assail his character. The bond of Christian love is stronger than the disagreement dividing you.

What was wrong with James and John lives on in most of us. We want to bully and domineer; so we cultivate the rapier thrust of sarcasm and learn how to be serenely obnoxious in a genteel way. Our skill at this sort of thing has produced one of the gravest weaknesses in Protestantism; we call it the sidewalk meeting. People are unwilling, sometimes afraid, to speak their minds in the meeting, and so they gather in tight little groups afterward, with all the pros under the elm tree passionately agreeing with each other and all the cons nodding sagely under the maple tree. Neither the pros nor the cons have the slightest intention of destroying the Church, but that's what can happen. I have known congregations to sever because dissident groups would not bring their disagreements to the proper place for open discussion.

After the argument comes the vote. Suppose the vote goes against you. Take it with a smile. You are a Christian. It is not your job to get your way all the time. But it is your job all the time to help the other person to be a Christian. A majority is not always right, but a chip on the shoulder is always wrong. We believe in a power making for the right. If you are genuinely right, then all eternity is on your side, and you can best hasten the victory of the right by acting like a Christian while the group catches up with you.

In the world, the leader is the one who gets his way. In the Church the real leader is the one who does things Jesus' way, not by commanding but by serving, putting God first, neighbors second, and self last.

7

THE CHURCH AND CIVIL AFFAIRS

Amos 5:21-24

Amos 5:21-24

I hate, I despise your feasts,
  and I take no delight in your solemn assemblies.
Even though you offer me your
  burnt offerings and cereal offerings,
  I will not accept them,
and the peace offerings of your fatted beasts
  I will not look upon.
Take away from me the noise of your songs;
  to the melody of your harps I will not listen.
But let justice roll down like waters,
  and righteousness like an ever-flowing stream.

7

THE CHURCH AND CIVIL AFFAIRS

Amos 5:21-24

The Church today is divided sharply, sometimes bitterly, about involvement in political matters. Government has entered what used to be the Church's business — welfare in the broadest sense — and now many are urging the Church to withdraw. Should Church leaders offer leadership about such matters as civil rights, collective bargaining, military affairs, and slum clearance? Some call such concern "meddling," others of us call it "evangelism."

WHERE IS CHRIST'S KINGDOM?

Remember always that Jesus said, "My kingdom is not of this world." Does this mean that we should let the world rot and busy ourselves only with "spiritual" affairs? This is not the example Jesus set. One point should have been settled long ago for Christians; let us not debate it: we seek an eternal Kingdom, not merely an improved society. I am not dusting off the old Social Gospel, which was sometimes more social than gospel. I am saying that concern about human welfare is inseparable from orthodox Christianity for two reasons: first, such concern is the only way we can proclaim the gospel to many of our neighbors, and second, such concern is implied in the gospel itself.

Merely political responses to the cry of pain will only change the location of the pain. Following a recent, tragic

97

riot, one man said to me, "These people have plenty of relief; what else do they want?" They want Christ. Most of them don't know it. How is the Church to tell them except by caring about the things they care about?

I agree completely with Thomas Merton who said, "To reconcile man with man and not with God is to reconcile no one at all." But there won't be much reconciling with God if the Church's message to the poor is: "'Go in peace, be warmed and filled,' without giving them the things needed for the body" (James 2:16).

Poor people sometimes accuse us, acidly, of plunging into social affairs as a gimmick to attract new members. If statistical growth is our motive, we deserve the acid. But let me ask a question of all Christians who live in comfortable homes, who have plenty to eat and excellent medical service and first class voting citizenship, whose children attend fine schools. Can we call ourselves Christian while ignoring our brothers — for whom Christ died — who lack what we are tempted to take for granted?

If the Church is the Body of Christ, then we are already in the midst of civil affairs. A Christian legislator, or judge, or union representative, or school teacher, or soldier, is a member of Christ's Body whenever and however he practices his faith on his job; and no one objects to this. But the cries are loud and shocked when a Church group offers constructive suggestions about public housing, or something of the sort. And when a minister gets out on a picket line, the cries turn into screams. Has the Carpenter of Nazareth quit caring what happens in the construction trades?

We ministers face a dilemma. Many want us to emerge from our comfortable studies long enough to administer soothing syrup to the congregation, then to slip back quietly. Their constant plea is, "Don't rock the boat." Our heavenly Father, however, seems to expect something quite different from us, if we may judge by what we profess to be His holy Word.

THE PROPHET AMOS

About 750 years before Jesus' time, a farmer who lived near Bethlehem went to Bethel, royal sanctuary in the Kingdom of Israel. It was a time of great prosperity (for the rich) and ostentatious luxury, somewhat like our own. Scholars used to think Amos' remark about ivory palaces a bit of oriental hyperbole, but in recent excavations archaeologists have found ivory slivers by the thousand. The wealthy nobles paneled their homes with ivory and sat around sipping cocktails wondering darkly what had gotten into the lower classes these days. Amos looked at Bethel, at the royal palace and the magnificent Temple. He saw the homes where the rich lived in luxury. He saw and smelled the slums. And then he preached a sermon. The book of Amos is short: in my Bible it is only eight pages. Dynamite comes in small packages, too. Amos' sermon was so explosive that he was invited to leave Bethel. Before leaving — if the present account reflects chronology — he preached another sermon more explosive than the first.

Amos is not the ideal upon whom a minister today should pattern his life and work. A minister usually hopes to be around next week to continue what he has started; he must persuade rather than blast. And Amos' more serious failing was his apparent lack of love. When these things have been said, the fact remains that the prophecy of Amos is part of the Holy Bible, and as such it is God's order to the Church.

THE MESSAGE OF AMOS

Two subjects fill Amos' brief prophecy: first, the glory of God, and second, the responsibility to our fellow man that must express our faith in God.

Amos wrote what many consider the finest Hebrew in the Old Testament, and with exquisitely sculptured poetry he radiates the divine glory in words that only Job and a few psalms can approach:

> He who made the Pleiades and Orion,
>   and turns deep darkness into the morning,
>   and darkens the day into night,
> and calls for the waters of the sea,
>   and pours them out upon the surface of the earth,
> — the Lord is his name.

The passage is one of several apostrophes where Amos stands in reverent awe before the sheer mystery and wonder of God. This apostrophe expresses three basics of faith: the Lord created the starry heavens, the Lord controls what happens on earth, and man knows something of the divine nature.

Orion and the Pleiades were created by God, and they don't know it. God calls for the waters of the sea and pours them on the earth, but neither the waters nor the earth know it. Yet we specks of dust who live on earth know who is our Creator, and we know His name. God's name, in Biblical usage, is more than the label; it means His character, His essential nature. Similar brief apostrophes are studded like stars in an otherwise somber sky; for the prophecy of Amos is anything but beautiful and enjoyable. The rest of the book deals with civil affairs, and the responsibility of faith to be involved in them.

THE RESPONSIBILITY OF FAITH

With rare tact, Amos begins his prophecy on a popular note: he criticizes someone else, Damascus. Then he turns his attention to Gaza, then to Tyre and to Edom. If you will take a map of Palestine and notice the different capitals that Amos condemns, you will find each a little closer to Bethel than was the former. The last to be mentioned is Jerusalem, close geographically and close spiritually.

The message in each case is the same. Damascus has sinned; Damascus will be judged. Gaza has sinned; Gaza will be judged. And so on. In most cases the sin is easily understandable today, and unless God has changed his mind, it is still sinful and still worthy of His divine judgment. Damascus, Edom, and Ammonites were excessively cruel in war. Gaza and Tyre enslaved their fellow men; the latter "did not remember the covenant of brotherhood."

People in ancient Israel, like us, derived a vicarious sense of righteousness from hearing their enemies denounced. Can you picture their glee when the strange prophet began to condemn Judah — haughty Judah with the stuck-up airs and all that fol-de-rol about the Holy Temple?

> For three transgressions of Judah,
>   and for four, I will not revoke the punishment;
> because they have rejected the law of the Lord,
>   and have not kept his statutes,
> but their lies have led them astray,
>   after which their fathers walked.

And now Amos has finished being tactful. He quits preaching and starts meddling, and I don't know how much closer to civil affairs a preacher could get.

> They sell the righteous for silver,
>   and the needy for a pair of shoes —
> they that trample the head of the
>   poor into the dust of the earth,
> and turn aside the way of the afflicted;
> a man and his father go in to the same maiden,
>   so that my holy name is profaned;
> they lay themselves down beside every altar
>   upon garments taken in pledge;
> and in the house of their God they drink
>   the wine of those who have been fined.

The sins listed have a curiously modern ring, and only one comes under the heading of individual morality: presumably even in ancient Bethel a few men did not visit the local prostitutes. Otherwise Amos is talking about the sort of thing we preachers are criticized for trying to correct today: exploiting the poor, lack of adequate social service for those who are in trouble, greedy loan-sharks and venal administration of justice.

The remark about garments taken in pledge may need a little clarification: we are familiar with the thing under discussion, we just describe it differently. Many people of ancient Palestine would have only one garment, a cloak, which by cruel necessity served as a blanket at night. So the Law contains a wise, compassionate provision:

> If ever you take your neighbor's garment in pledge, you shall restore it to him before the sun goes down; for that is his only covering, it is his mantle for his body; in what else shall he sleep?

> Exodus 22:26-27.

Amos pictures law enforcement: the money-lender takes the cloak in pledge, he imbibes freely in the Temple, and lies down on the poor man's cloak for a pleasant, drunken night, while his neighbor catches pneumonia. Religious practice has no connection with love for God or neighbor.

Bethel was a very religious city. The Temple was big business. Of course, the ancient faith had been slightly diluted; Jeroboam set up a golden calf there and in general tailored the faith to fit the modern mind. As a result, the Temple was crowded. The music was magnificent. The treasury was over-flowing. In every sense, except one, religion had it made; God had a good image; the Church was a success. The lonely herdsman from Tekoa thought the one exception rather important.

> Prepare to meet your God, O Israel!
> For lo, he who forms the mountains,
>   and creates the wind,
> and declares to man what is his thought;
> who makes the morning darkness,
>   and treads on the heights of the earth —
> the Lord, the God of hosts is his name!

What use is the most powerful cannon ever made, if it points in the wrong direction? What use is all our religious apparatus, if it does not aim us toward our destiny with God?

GOD CARES ABOUT THE POOR

God was, in ancient times where it doesn't hurt us, deeply concerned about the poor. Does He no longer care? I have heard Christians — they called themselves — oppose programs designed to help poor people out of their misery because Jesus said, "The poor you have with you always." These same people can learnedly discuss the hideous way the ancient Pharisees evaded the Law, but they can't, or won't, bring the discussion close to home. Somewhere around one-half the world's people are suffering from malnutrition today. We need not worry that our efforts to correct specific dangers will leave nothing for our children to act Christian about. Why did Amos care about the poor? Because he cared deeply about God.

I have discovered, to my horror, that whenever I mention concern for the poor, people immediately conclude that I am endorsing the Federal government's welfare program; so let me make abundantly clear that I am talking about you, not your Uncle, and then let me make a few remarks about government and welfare, directed both to my friends who believe that the government can do nothing right, and the others who believe that the answer to every question should be sought in Washington.

In the United States about one-fifth of the people are officially classed as poverty-stricken. The various agencies of government, with considerable urging from the Church, have provided welfare programs, which have aroused much wrath from some Christians, who can point with devastating accuracy toward grave and tragic abuses — chief among them that some families are now entering the fourth generation on relief.

The dole is an emergency measure. When people come to depend on it as a way of life, something is horribly wrong, not only with those who accept it but with those who pay it. As we criticize welfare policies that permit some to live parasitically, we aren't criticizing only the lazy poor, we are also criticizing us stupid rich people who haven't — to date — thought up anything better than continuing a program that is not to the best interests of the person on the dole, the taxpayer, the employer, the police department, the Church, or anyone else.

The trouble is not that the Church has meddled too much in civil affairs; the trouble is that we have dabbled in the shallows when we should be swimming in the depths. Government can, and should, act to relieve specific, pressing emergencies. Government cannot love, and should not attempt to. That's supposed to be our job. We are supposed to help people find meaning in life. We are supposed to guide them toward such worthy goals as personal responsibility. We are supposed to help, and let "ordinary men" do the condemning.

The Church should be ready, willing, and able to prod the legislature when necessary to meet a particular situation. If that is meddling in civil affairs, then we'd better meddle. But if we are the Church, the Body of Christ, we will recognize the limits to what government can do, and the harm that can come from too much government activity.

Some matters can be handled better by all of us working together — government — than by individuals. I don't know anyone who would willingly turn the United States Navy back to individual enterprise. We tried it, during the Revolution, and found difficulty in telling the difference between a privateer and a pirate. And so we might consider each item of the welfare program, asking if this is something the government ought to handle or if the government ought to stay out of it. My own opinion runs from ardent support to violent opposition, depending upon the project under discussion. Since I am not now discussing government, I shall not delve into the minutiae. But I will express one highly personal conclusion: the more I see of government in action, the more impressed I am with the importance of the individual. The more I watch City Hall trying to solve people's problems, the happier I am when individuals or community groups try to solve their own problems.

For example: recently a group of us met in Miami with a great-hearted man who is chairman of the committee that is trying to coordinate the many public and private efforts to relieve specific needs. He was generous with praise for all that our Church groups have done, and he pointed with candid charity to some things we have done wrong. He told about a Cuban refugee who leased a filling-station and pumped a great deal of gasoline, enough to bring him a personal income of almost a thousand dollars a month. Yet he came to the Small Loans Administration — a government project — for funds to forestall bankruptcy. Instead of writing a check, the civil servant in charge asked a Christian friend who knows the gasoline business to visit the station. During the discussion, the business man asked to see the Cuban's books. He looked startled and asked, "What books?" At a point like this most volunteers give up. But the Christian business man stayed with it. He taught the Cuban how to keep books, and, just as important, how to interpret them. Today the Cuban is a successful business man, not another drain upon the public welfare, and all because a Christian

acted his faith. Is this Christian outreach? Not if it ends
with a business failure turned into a business success. A
retail merchant's central need, now and always, is for God,
not mere finances. Is there a better way of introducing a
man to God than caring about the man and his immediate
needs?

The welfare state has produced ills along with the ills it
has alleviated. It used to be, when people lived in small
communities where everyone knew everyone else, that the
richer people took a personal interest in those who lacked.
We can make nasty remarks about Lady Bountiful if we
want to, and we can talk about the evil of paternalism. The
old system had weakness; so does the new. Now we automatically assume that government will take care of everything,
and sometimes we are grossly incorrect. We still need responsible, concerned individuals.

Not far from our Church is a small, seldom-used passage-
way leading from a street to an alley. The police ambulance
was called there because an elderly woman was lying on the
sidewalk, unconscious. While the police were gently lifting
her to the stretcher, a man at the window of an adjacent
boarding-house stopped picking his teeth long enough to
say, "I wondered when you'd come. She's been there two
days."

We who live in cities simply can't know one another; it's
physically impossible. And so we can easily slide into a comfortable frame of mind that the welfare state will meet
all the needs. It's easy not to worry about misery, providing
it's the other fellow who is miserable. That's what God
is talking about through Amos: comfortable people who don't
know or care what's going on in the world.

> Hear this word, you cows of Bashan,
>   who are in the mountain of Samaria,
> who oppress the poor, who crush the needy,
>   who say to their husbands,
>   "Bring, that we may drink!"
>
> Woe to those who are at ease in Zion,
>   and to those who feel secure on the
>   mountain of Samaria.

> Woe to those who lie upon beds of ivory,
>> and stretch themselves upon their couches,
> and eat lambs from the flock,
>> and calves from the midst of the stall;
> who sing idle songs to the sound of the harp . . .
> who drink wine in bowls,
>> and anoint themselves with the finest oils,
>> but are not grieved over the ruin of Joseph!

The smugly comfortable come to the Lord's house and listen critically to the lovely music, and the Lord says to them through the fiery prophet:

> I hate, I despise your feasts,
>> and I take no delight in your solemn assemblies,
> Even though you offer me your
>> burnt offerings and cereal offerings,
>> I will not accept them,
> and the peace offerings of your fatted beasts
>> I will not look upon.
> Take away from me the noise of your songs;
>> to the melody of your harps I will not listen.
> But let justice roll down like waters,
>> and righteousness like an everflowing stream.

Do you suppose He has changed His mind?

WHAT'S TO DO?

The Church ought to be concerned about people who are living in misery. Senator Abraham A. Ribicoff, who is no foe of the welfare state, recently told some Church leaders:

> Stop looking at lists of program and begin looking at people.
> . . . You can help bridge the incredible chasm between the institutions of our society and the people who need help the most. Whether those institutions are government clinics or absentee landlords, they have become concerned with the mass and unrelated to the individual. You can help put a face on the invisible man.

In order to put a face on the invisible man, you must first know him. That's the Church's job, which we are performing with indifferent success.

When you know a person, then you begin to understand the kind of thing he is worried about. When you know a Negro as an individual, you find that he is concerned about voting rights and job opportunities for his people. When you know a migrant laborer, you learn that he cares about schooling for his children. If you had to ride on the busses he rides, you would be disturbed about bald tires too. When you know people who live in the slums, you find them quite interested in garbage collection and violence on the streets. Should the Church be concerned about such matters? Amos was. Jesus was.

One person, all by himself, can't do much to correct any of the conditions mentioned. A lot of people, working together, can move mountains. A lot of people working together are called a union, a civil-rights group, a community-action council, or something like that. It is hard to see why some Christians object to such organizations. They all got the idea from us. A whole lot of people working together to carry out the will of Christ is called a congregation.

Christian leaders are condemned bitterly for involvement in civil activities. Those who do the condemning say correctly that man's primary need is not political or economic, but spiritual. Having said it, those with the loudest voices show no shadow of a sign of concern about the political and economic realities with which their fellowmen are living. If they have any constructive ideas about these secondary matters, they keep them thoroughly out of sight. The poor people in the United States, and most of the European countries, decided a long time ago that the Church doesn't really care about them.

CHRISTIAN SOCIAL ACTION

The Church today contains Christians who love Christ so much that they are willing to endure the scorn of their fellow Christians and enter deeply into the lives of the poor and the oppressed — exactly as Jesus urged us to do. They think this is evangelism, the Christian words that the poor can hear.

To keep this discussion a comfortable distance away from home (I have learned a few things from Amos) I refer you to the worker-priest movement in France. In 1944 a group of Roman Catholic priests, led by a deep and Christ-like concern about the gap between the poor and the Church, left the security of their parishes or schools or monasteries, and plunged fully into the working man's life. They worked at factory benches or drove trucks or engaged in some other form of labor for their support. They learned to their chagrin how great was the gap, how the poor mistrusted and feared them because they represented the smug middle-class Church. They found that before they could be accepted as representatives of Christ they must first be accepted as men. Gradually, over a long period, most of them were accepted.

As the worker-priests entered more and more fully into the working-man's life, they began to see the world from a different perspective. They began to sympathize with, rather than just talk about, the worker's desire to be accepted as a man, not a production unit. And this meant activity in the union. At the time there was a "safe" union, with which the few Roman Catholic working-men affiliated. And there was a "radical" union which seemed more interested in helping the worker than in being respectable. After a year or two of practical experience, the priests without exception turned their backs on the safe union and affiliated in one way or another with the radical, where their education and experience in group leadership channeled many into office, or promoted them to be union spokesmen. They were surprised to find themselves as strike-leaders, and some encountered trouble with the police, which inevitably brought rumblings in Rome.

In 1954 Pope Pius XII stopped the worker-priest movement, and ordered the participants to return to their customary priestly duties. Rather than obey, almost 40 per cent of the men involved left the priesthood. These were not professional malcontents and trouble-makers. Several were highly respected as scholars, several had received significant promotions in the recent past. All believed that their Church had betrayed the poor by refusing to understand their needs. (I am happy to say that under Pope Paul the movement has been started again, with wise [perhaps over-wise] provision against abuse of a spiritual mission.)

I am not uncritically endorsing "radical" unions. I am illustrating only one thing: when you look at the world through a poor man's eyes, you do not see what a rich man sees. Jesus saw the world through a poor man's eyes. Does His Church?

Recently *The National Observer* ran a news story about some Protestant clergymen who have left the ministry with congregations to help people in the Philadelphia slums make real our pledge, ". . . with liberty and justice to all." The group has announced at least one operating principle that should be inscribed in fire upon the heart of every Church spokesman: before producing the answers, they are trying to find out what the questions are.

The news story, instead of giving a mass of statistics, describes vividly one young minister who, after years of working with a congregation, now works at City Hall all day and at night visits the slum areas, showing people how to assume the responsibilities of citizenship. (Some slum-dwellers have given up hope. Society, rightly or wrongly, has given up hope for these people, abandoning them to what illusory consolation they can find in liquor, drugs, sex, and violence. I do not say these people are beyond helping, though I frequently feel that way. By and large the fellow you can help is the one who wants to help himself. If he doesn't know how to go about it you can give him a real boost up the ladder by showing him what to do. And this boost is part of Christian evangelism.)

Two sentences in the article disturbed me deeply. One was a question by an unnamed minister: "But who can identify this as God's work?"

Christians everywhere recognize their privilege and duty to deal with the results of slum life: to feed the hungry, to provide medical care for the sick, to visit the imprisoned, and so on. Is it not likewise the Church's privilege and duty to correct evil conditions at their source, when that lies within our power?

I do not propose that our responsibility has ended when we have straightened up the garbage-collection system in the slums. The slum-dweller, like the rest of us, does not live by bread alone. I propose instead that we Christians who live in attractive, well-kept neighborhoods be concerned about

everything that concerns our brothers who live in filthy,
disease-ridden neighborhoods. Their first concern ought to
be with God. If it happens to be with garbage, then maybe
that's the best possible place to meet them with the message
that God cares, and His Church cares.

The other sentence that hit me between the eyes was
spoken by the young minister-turned-civil-servant. He said,
"For my fellow Christians in City Hall the Church is always
somewhere else — Rome, the suburbs, in one's memories of
childhood, but never in the downtown office." The comment
exposes three fallacies of today's Church life.

First: that the Church is one thing and daily life another.
Many who work in the office at City Hall are Church members. They do not seem to realize that they are just as much
the Church on Tuesday as they are on Sunday. Jesus Christ
wants to be in City Hall. That's why His Body is there.

Second: that the minister is the Church. This one nettles
me. I am a member of the Church: the left elbow, perhaps,
or some other ungraceful but necessary organ in Christ's Body.
You too are members: you are Christ's hands, His feet, His
eyes and ears and tongue. If your daily work is in City Hall,
then that and your home are the most important places in the
world for you to discharge your Christian faith. What you do
here is important only if it is reflected in what you do there.

The third fallacy that gets me down is the idea that the
Church can be the only major organization in town that is not
concerned about the things Jesus was concerned about.

I wish those who so readily criticize Christian social action
groups would examine carefully just what they are saying.
Continue to look for a moment at the minister-turned-civil-
servant. He dedicated his life to Christ. Then, in order to do
the sort of thing Jesus did, he thought it necessary to leave
the Church that Jesus put on earth to do it. He accepted the
limitations of political office, which must be religiously neutral,
because he felt his Church was not really, passionately concerned about people who are troubled by rats and syphilis
and high rents and low wages.

I do not question the motives of my colleague who left the
pulpit to become a civil-servant, but I do not plan to follow
his example. I know many clergymen who have discovered

that the work of the organized Church is incredibly difficult, and have left the pastoral ministry in defeat. I do not sense this defeat in the news story about the minister who sought another way to serve his Lord; instead I sense a call from Christ which he obeyed. But Christ has not issued such a call to me.

While my colleague is in the office or in the slums, he is one man, valiantly representing Christ. When I am in the pulpit, I am in a position to influence hundreds. Do not remind me of my failure, I am more conscious of them than you are. Let me remind you of the hundreds who worship here, and then translate their worship into Christian service, in this community and throughout the world.

It happens, at this moment, a member who recently left our congregation is working in the Philadelphia slums. The love of Christ led her there. I do not claim any individual credit for the decision that led this Christian woman to dedicate her skills to poor people, but the Church I serve gets much credit. At this moment a man from our congregation is working with social outcasts in Australia. A man from our Church is trying to help those who live in the slums of Manila, where conditions are even worse than they are in Philadelphia. Another of our members is teaching a Sunday School class in Liberia while her husband is helping the government straighten out its finances.

Here at home members of our congregation are involved in every significant effort for community betterment, and, even more important, many of them go far out of their way to help individual poor people finance a mortgage, or get a better job, or attend the right school, or fix the plumbing. For example, one man in the real estate business was asked to sell a house. He took hours of his valuable time, and incidentally talked himself out of a legitimate commission, to persuade his client that she could not afford to sell. It costs her less to live in the house than it would in any possible rented quarters. He is engaged in a tough, competitive business, but he tries to act like a Christian while he is working at it.

Your dollar for benevolence extends the concern of your Church into the barrios of Rio and the turbulent reaches of the upper Nile. Your Church is speaking for you in the jungles

of Yucatan, the Congo, and Ceylon. Your Church is at Point
Barrow, Alaska, which is as far north as we can get. Wherever
we go, we do what is necessary, as the rational way to
express God's love. We who know something about bacteria
could not, in conscience, withhold our knowledge of sanita-
tion from people whom we profess to love. The hospital, the
school, and the agricultural experiment station are adjuncts
to the Christian mission, wherever we go. And where it is
possible, we help people to a better economic life. We do not
pretend that this is a substitute for spiritual life. Neither do
we dwell in the never-never land where spiritual things can
be divorced from groceries and mosquito control and 30 per
cent interest rates. Because we love Christ, we love the people He died to save.

I am trying to be a Christian. Because I care deeply about
God, I care deeply about people, particularly those in need.
If I thought I could help people more effectively by leaving
the pastoral ministry and going into government work — I
have only one life and I want to make that one count — I
would go where I thought I could accomplish the most.
That's why I'm here. As I see it, the highest service I can
perform for my neighbor who is in bitter economic or social
need is to hold up to you the living Christ, not the weak,
sissified Jesus of so much popular theology, but the fighter who
lost His life in the battle for justice, and yet He lives today
and calls you to be His agent to make this His world.

8

THE FUTURE OF
RELIGIONLESS CHRISTIANITY

Ezekiel 40:1-5

Ezekiel 40:1-5

In the twenty-fifth year of our exile, at the beginning of the year, on the tenth day of the month, in the fourteenth year after the city was conquered, on that very day, the hand of the Lord was upon me, and brought me in the visions of God into the land of Israel, and set me down upon a very high mountain, on which was a structure like a city opposite me. When he brought me there, behold, there was a man, whose appearance was like bronze, with a line of flax and a measuring reed in his hand; and he was standing in the gateway. And the man said to me, "Son of man, look with your eyes, and hear with your ears, and set your mind upon all that I shall show you, for you were brought here in order that I might show it to you; declare all that you see to the house of Israel."

And behold, there was a wall all around the outside of the temple area, and the length of the measuring reed in the man's hand was six long cubits, each being a cubit and a handbreadth in length; so he measured the thickness of the wall, one reed; and the height, one reed.

(And so for several pages, that picture the future Temple as remarkably like the Temple of the past.)

8

THE FUTURE OF
RELIGIONLESS CHRISTIANITY

Ezekiel 40:1-5

Dietrich Bonhoeffer, the German martyr, has been elected involuntary spokesman for the shrill contemporary theologians who are willing to scrap the organized Church and all the rest of traditional Christianity. They have pounced joyously upon Bonhoeffer's phrase "religionless Christianity" in their laudable zeal to discard the trivia from our faith. Thomas Altizer, who has decided that God is among the discardable items, says:

> One of the most important sources of a new direction of theology will be a new and more critical understanding of the uniqueness of Christianity. All theological talk about a "religionless Christianity" will remain largely meaningless so long as the theologian remains ignorant of the historical phenomenon of religion.

I usually do not know quite what Mr. Altizer means, but I hazard an opinion that he thinks the creative direction of contemporary theology is toward "religionless Christianity." I join him in urging all Christians to study Church history and the non-Christian religions. After one has trod where others have trod, one begins to realize that the way has been travelled before. Ever since there have been Christians someone has been trying to destroy the Church, and it is still here, still helping people to find their way in the dark, still relevant to daily life.

Ezekiel was the Biblical prophet who lived and worked in a time when the religious forms he knew and loved had been scrapped. The Temple was razed. The holy altar was destroyed. The priests were scattered or slaughtered. Ezekiel lived with the reality of "religionless Judaism," and he saw prophetically that the spirit of faith needs some kind of forms to hold it together. These forms are the externals, what we call "religion."

Ezekiel's "religion" was demolished; so he helped to design the interim forms that held faith together, and was the principal architect, known to us at least, for the new forms that developed. The new "religion" differed radically from the old, yet there was more continuity than change. I pray that the Church tomorrow may differ radically from the Church today, but I do not expect the Christian "religion" — the outward forms through which we express the inward faith — to disappear from the world, not until the gates of hell have caved in.

DIETRICH BONHOEFFER

Dietrich Bonhoeffer indubitably made famous the phrase "religionless Christianity," which some contemporary theologians have enthusiastically adopted as their spring-board into nihility. It would be hard to overstate my admiration for Dietrich Bonhoeffer, or to tell how much I have benefited from studying his work. I revere him both as a scholar and as a martyr who gave his life for Christ. Not least among the qualities I admire is Bonhoeffer's freedom from the sloppy sentiment that weakens modern Christianity. I encounter some gristle in his thoughts but little fat.

Dietrich Bonhoeffer was born in 1906, the son of a prominent psychiatrist. When he was only twenty-one he presented a masterful thesis at Berlin University, *Sanctorum Communio*. (Those who have read the thesis will not need to be told how much I owe to Dietrich Bonhoeffer.) He served briefly as a pastor in Germany, then, following a year's theological studies in the United States, he began teaching. His most influential book, while he lived, was *The Cost of Discipleship*, written in 1937.

In 1939 Dietrich Bonhoeffer visited the United States as a lecturer, while his beloved Fatherland was skidding to inevitable destruction. He had many offers to remain in this country, but he rejected them, and returned to Germany on one of the last ships before war was declared. The next few years he spent working with the Confessing Church, writing his unfinished masterpiece *Ethics*, and aiding the German Resistance movement. The Nazis arrested him in 1943 and hanged him in 1945.

Today, the most influential among all Dietrich Bonhoeffer's works are the *Letters and Papers from Prison*, edited by Eberhard Bethge, to whom many of the letters were addressed. Here one finds the sparks kindled by the clash between flint and steel, the flint being Bonhoeffer's own brilliant personality and the steel an alloy compounded of Nazi brutality and total indifference to God among many fellow prisoners.

In one of his fascinating letters Dietrich Bonhoeffer names the intellectual leaders who have led man to believe that he does not need God as a "working hypothesis." (Certainly I do not need, or want, a "working hypothesis" in heaven.) It began with Herbert of Cherbury, who claimed that reason, without revelation, gives valid religious knowledge. Montaigne substituted moral principles for the divine commandments. Machiavelli set politics free from morality. Grotius claimed that international law is a law of nature. Descartes taught a form of deism, that the world is a mechanism running with no intervention from God. Spinosa, the pantheist, identified God with nature. Then Nicholas of Cusa and Giordano Bruno taught that space is infinite. (The religious authorities of the time saw, correctly, that if the universe is infinite then it was not created. I think they were wrong in condemning the idea as heretical; Christians should not be afraid to examine anything.) Feuerbach eliminated God as a "working hypothesis" from religion and philosophy.

To my surprise Bonhoeffer did not mention three men whose work has generated much theological thought in the United States. One was Charles Lyell, the geologist who taught that the earth's surface was shaped by the slow opera-

tion of natural forces working over aeons, and not in a few
catastrophes. Charles Darwin forced the Church to rethink
the question about man's body, and Sigmund Freud is still
making us re-examine the human soul.

Everyone is familiar, in a general way, with the trend.
Man has reached a place where he thinks he can function
without God. And what's to do? Dietrich Bonhoeffer turns
his back on the "emergency exits" that have been proposed,
chief among them the retreat to the Middle Ages. He says:

> It reminds one of the song:
>
> *It's a long way back to the land of childhood,*
> *But if only I knew the way!*
>
> There isn't any such way, at any rate not at the cost of
> deliberately abandoning our intellectual sincerity. The only
> way is that of Matthew 18:3 [Unless you turn and become
> like little children, you will never enter the kingdom of God.]
> i.e., through repentance, through *ultimate* honesty.

From his cell Dietrich Bonhoeffer wrote to the man who,
he believed, could most help him to clarify his thought:

> What *is* Christianity, and indeed what *is* Christ, for us to-
> day? The time when men could be told everything by means
> of words, whether theological or simply pious, is over, and
> so is the time of inwardness and conscience, which is to say
> the time of religion as such. We are proceeding towards a
> time of no religion at all. . . . If we reach the stage of being
> radically without religion – and I think this is more or less
> the case already . . . what does that mean for "Christianity"?
> . . . How can Christ become the Lord even of those with no
> religion? If religion is no more than the garment of Chris-
> tianity – and even that garment has had very different aspects
> at different periods – then what is a religionless Christianity?
> . . . How do we speak of God without religion, i.e., without
> the temporally-influenced presuppositions of metaphysics, in-
> wardness, and so on?

Nobody, I believe, could question that many today are
"radically without religion." How can the Church speak to
them? I find that words like "sin," "redemption," and even
"God" are simply meaningless to many of my friends. It isn't

that they disbelieve; they just don't know what I'm talking about. In order to talk with them, must I drag in philosophic ideas from ancient Greece that are now part of the Christian religion? (I believe the classic expression of the Holy Trinity is true, but I'm afraid that I do not accept the idea of substance upon which our expression of the doctrine is built. And, I hazard a guess, you don't accept that idea of substance either. Further, although I claim no expertise about customs in heaven, I am fairly sure that the angels and archangels do not address the Deity as "Consubstantial Unity of three co-eternal Hypostases.")

A central idea running through Bonhoeffer's work is the reality of God as revealed in Jesus Christ. This reality is disclosed in part through the Church, which is not something sacred in an otherwise secular world. Indeed Bonhoeffer erases the line between sacred and secular, because Christ came to reconcile the world to God — a thought that is developed with even greater penetration than Bonhoeffer's by the Apostle Paul in his letter to the Ephesians.

Work, family, and government are, like the Church, agencies through which Christ reveals the heavenly Father's will to the world. This is profound Biblical Christianity; following the Lord's crucifixion the veil of the Temple was rent. So we can recognize that all of God's creation is holy; but that does not require us to down-grade what the Savior founded because He thought we needed it, the organized Church.

A great many aspects of contemporary religion could well be sacrificed, and we all would be richer. I would nominate for quick oblivion all bake-sales, rummage-sales, and other money-making gimmicks that detour Christian stewardship. I would swoon for joy if the end were announced of all prizes, banners, awards, pins, medallions and other trinkets given for good attendance. Our "star" system among the clergy is deplorable even by Hollywood standards. And those meetings where the program consists of people wondering why people stay away from meetings where the program consists of people wondering why people stay from meetings where. . . . I wish we could eliminate about half the hymns in the book, including both those that are unsingable and those

not worth singing. The tinsel with which we desecrate the
Cross could well be sacrificed to the glory of God.

On a more serious note, I turn to one outspoken critic,
Pierre Berton, who explains in *The Comfortable Pew* why he
left the Church, which has been pushing people away from
God by our attachment to incomprehensible concepts, words,
and procedures.

Mr. Berton tells, with bewilderment, about his plans
to have his first daughter baptized in the Anglican communion.
Rightly, he studied the order of service for the Publick Baptism of Infants, and found that he could not, without hypocrisy, take part in it. The phrase "all men are conceived and
born in sin" stuck in his craw; for he thought it meant that
the God-given beauty of married love is sinful, and that a
tiny child is guilty of actual sin. (Mr. Berton is not the first
to be confused by the idea of original sin.) And he adds:

> Since that experience, a variety of enlightened priests have
> indicated to me that this passage does not really mean what
> it seems to mean. . . . All the passage is said to have meant
> is that we are all imperfect in the sight of God. Perhaps that
> is so. But if it *was* so; if that was what the Church really
> believed; if the passage that I was required to attest to in
> this most sacred moment meant something other than what it
> seemed to mean, why — in the name of that God who was
> being invoked — why was not all this stated in the clearest
> possible English? If the priests of the Church themselves
> did not believe the literal truth of what they were saying,
> why were they required to say it?

The Church today is encumbered with baggage from the
past that seriously interfered with our ability to speak to the
present; hence the need for "religionless Christianity." I am a
living witness that sometimes the Church, without calling upon
yesterday's vocabulary, manages to communicate with people
who know nothing about God. For example, a young man I
know is now in the penitentiary, serving a sentence for armed
robbery. I am honored that this man calls me a friend.
More important, he calls Jesus Christ a friend. He would flunk
the most elementary examination in the Christian religion,
which doesn't worry me a bit, because he could give lessons

in faith to some theological professors I know. He has taken the first steps on the road to eternal life.

My young friend started becoming a Christian because a few Christ-like people cared enough to be his friends at a time when he most needed friendship — immediately after his arrest. They did not use the religious apparatus of the organized Church: no hymn-books, no theological tomes, no saw-dust trail. (Our jail offers meagre facilities for public worship.) They just acted like friends, not ignoring past failings, but hoping for the man who could grow to replace the criminal. Because they cared, my friend began for the first time in his life to think seriously about Jesus Christ. That's where I came into the picture, and for a purely mechanical reason: as a clergyman I can visit the jail more or less regularly, and I am allowed to correspond with my many friends in the penitentiary. They could do neither.

"Religionless Christianity" has turned my friend toward Jesus Christ. And what shall I do? Leave him in his present "religionless" state? I don't quite see it that way. I'm trying to help him to learn to pray and to read the Bible with discernment. I'm not throwing Christian theology at him in one big lump, but I am trying to introduce him to the great concepts of faith, one at a time. I am encouraging him to work and worship with the prison Chaplain — a man I know well, though we have never met. When he is released, I hope that he will become a part of the Christian Church, and that he will sing hymns and pray and reach out in Christian love to other people who don't understand the Christian vocabulary.

As I read Dietrich Bonhoeffer, it seems to me that he is urging Christlike concern toward people who don't understand Christianity, or care about it. He calls it "religionless Christianity." I don't much care what you call it; it's the best way — the only way — I know to reach a great many of our neighbors today.

You can find help and strength for daily life in most of Dietrich Bonhoeffer's work, which is so permeated with traditional Christian ideas that the far-out theologians find it embarrassing. So they have conveniently divided him into the early, middle, and late Bonhoeffer, and have clutched to the heart some late writings of God's saint and martyr.

Shortly before the end, Dietrich Bonhoeffer wrote that his great unfinished task was to complete *Ethics,* which would lead one to believe that he still subscribed to some key thoughts in the masterful study. He said in his letters that his thoughts were changing. Everybody changes. But I seriously doubt that he was quite so unstable as some of his disciples try to make him sound. And this is what Dr. Bonhoeffer had to say about the Church in the work that Adolph Hitler would not allow him to finish:

> The Church's word to the world is the word of the incarnation of God, of the love of God for the world in the sending of His Son, and of God's judgement upon unbelief. The word of the Church is the call to conversion, the call to belief in the love of God in Christ, and the call to preparation for Christ's second coming and for the future kingdom of God. It is, therefore, the word of redemption for all mankind.

If this is religionless Christianity, I'm for it.

Now look at the picture. Here is a Christian scholar to whom the Church — by and large — means the state Church. He sees the anti-Christ ruling the State, and gradually smothering the Church. (It is strange that Protestants who bewail the Church's intrusion into politics are loud to denounce Pope Pius XI for his failure to warn Italians against the war in Ethiopia, and Pope Pius XII for his silence about Nazi atrocities.) Among German Protestants were a few incredibly brave persons who spoke up for Christ and human freedom, against Adolph Hitler. The majority did what many now are urging the Church to do in the United States today — they preached a personal gospel and left politics to the politicians. And many sold their souls to become "German Christians," who docilely baptized Hitler's blasphemy.

Several years before the tragedy reached its climax, Dietrich Bonhoeffer prophetically wrote:

> A withdrawal of the Church from the world . . . would necessarily lead to the most drastic consequences, which are described in Revelation 13.

The prophecy — both John's and Bonhoeffer's — was fulfilled in the minutest detail. The Church withdrew. The beast arose and made war upon the saints, but was not quite victorious; for God saved a remnant of the faithful.

Dietrich Bonhoeffer was in prison. And where was the Church he had known and loved? Buildings had been padlocked and bombed into rubble. Individuals had stood up to be counted — and hanged. The organization had not been strong enough to prevent the rise of a power that almost destroyed decency, humanity, morality, and in the process, the Church.

Before the event, Dietrich Bonhoeffer wrote, and again I can but say prophetically:

> In Soloviev's story of the Anti-Christ, in the last days before Christ's return, the heads of the persecuted churches discuss the question of what is for each of them the most precious thing in Christianity; the decisive answer is that the most precious thing in Christianity is Jesus Christ Himself. . . . He is the center and the strength of the Bible, of the Church, and of theology, but also of humanity, of reason, of justice, and of culture. Everything must return to Him; it is only under His protection that it can live.

Here is a man whose home, security, and future have been stripped away. He has seen the failure of many friends within the Church he loves: a few openly betraying their Lord for a handful of silver, many denying their Lord more by silence than by word, and many fleeing from the safety that is nowhere except with Him. The State has failed. All the institutions of free society have failed. The Church has failed. But Christ is with him. Christ is more important and is stronger than any of the earthly institutions through which He customarily speaks to the world. Under these circumstances Bonhoeffer wrote about "religionless Christianity."

Dietrich Bonhoeffer's ideas are exciting to many, disturbing to some. It is only fair to allow him the last word about the expression he coined. While he was in prison he wrote a rough outline for a book in which he hoped to explore the implications of "religionless Christianity." And I quote, with enthusiastic approval, his own outline for the concluding section:

The Church is her true self only when she exists for humanity.
As a fresh start she should give away all her endowments
to the poor and needy. The clergy should live solely on the
free-will offerings of their congregations, or possibly engage
in some secular calling. She must take her part in the social
life of the world, not lording it over men, but helping and
serving them. She must tell men, whatever their calling,
what it means to live in Christ, to exist for others. And in
particular, our own Church will have to take a strong line
with the blasphemies of *hybris,* power-worship, envy and
humbug, for these are the roots of evil. She will have to
speak of moderation, purity, confidence, loyalty, steadfastness,
patience, discipline, humility, content and modesty. She
must not underestimate the importance of human example,
which has its origin in the humanity of Jesus, and which
is so important in the teaching of St. Paul. *It is not abstract
argument, but concrete example which gives her word emphasis and power.*

AND NOW, EZEKIEL

Ezekiel lived and worked in Babylon at a time when Nebuchadnezzar had done to the Jews everything that Hitler tried
to do to the Christians. Nebuchadnezzar had smashed the
Temple, torn down the altar, razed the city Jerusalem, and
totally disrupted Hebrew religious institutions. A few Jewish
people were exiled in Babylon, where they were free to work
at their several trades and to make what plans they could
for the future, as long as they created no disturbance. Under-
standably, many were cynical and bitter. They made clever
remarks about the death of God — though they did not use that
exact phrase. Under these circumstances, God called Ezekiel
to plan the future development of the Hebrew people.

All the scaffolding had been taken away from Ezekiel's
faith; music gone, ritual gone, hierarchy gone, Temple gone,
altar gone, everything gone — everything. But God met Ezekiel beside the River Chebar and announced clearly that
He would fulfill His promise to Abraham.

Ezekiel's strange prophecy is divided into halves. The
first, which doesn't concern us at the moment, tells about
divine judgment and human destruction. Then the destroyer
was Nebuchadnezzar; today he is Hitler, Stalin, Mao — we

suffer from no dearth of applicants. What we want is a word about the direction we should go in a time when nations are crumbling and beliefs are crumbling. Ezekiel provides this word in the latter half of his book, where he says that God is still in charge of history, and our task is to get on with the business of living with Him and for Him where we are and not where we would like to be.

The last eight chapters in Ezekiel are the strangest part of a strange book, where the prophet looks into the future and gives first a detailed architectural drawing of a Temple, and then a civil engineer's layout of Palestine and its capital city, Jerusalem. And my point is that the new Jerusalem closely resembles the old. Ezekiel foresaw changes, lots of them, but he foresaw more similarity than change.

The old institutions were smashed. Ezekiel was living with religionless Hebrew faith. He need not look far ahead to see that some kind of institution was needful for the present as plans were developing for the future. And so, while it was not possible to worship in the Temple — there was no Temple — Ezekiel helped to devise a new institution, the synagogue: a place for prayer and study and friendship, which did not house an altar. From the beginning Hebrew religion had been expressed through an altar. During the exile God taught his people that faith must never center upon a thing, no matter how good the thing may be. Faith must center upon God alone. We gather, from a few bewildering passages, that Ezekiel sternly opposed building an altar in Babylon. Yet for the long pull, over the centuries, Ezekiel, who helped to develop the altarless synagogue, foresaw a return to the ancient religious institution, the Temple, with its stately ritual and its unending sacrificial ceremony.

Ezekiel had good reason for believing that faith requires visible institutions. You have heard about the ten lost tribes of Israel. They weren't lost; they just fizzled out. In 722, a century and three-quarters before Ezekiel's time, the Assyrians besieged and conquered Samaria, the capital city of the ten northern tribes. The surviving Israelites were scattered in exile. The institutions of faith were demolished. The ten tribes lost their social cohesion and ultimately their faith.

All about him, Ezekiel saw the same thing happening to his fellow-exiles.

We need some kind of organization for our noblest spiritual impulses. It may be as free and spontaneous as the Society of Friends, or it may be as structured as the Salvation Army — to name two very different groups that have alike taken seriously our Savior's call to concern about human need. But without something to hold faith together, sooner or later it falls apart.

Ezekiel was a true conservative, who had one strong reason for believing that something might work in the future: it had worked in the past. Yet Ezekiel was no reactionary, in love with the past. He retained good traditions, but he smashed bad traditions left and right. The most meaningful changes — to us — were in what we call Church-state relationships. Before Ezekiel's time the Temple was more or less the royal chapel. Theoretically holiness from the Temple permeated the palace. In practice, harem intrigues and princes' knavery sullied the high altar. So Ezekiel drew a bold design for the Temple, and around it he built a massive wall, with the royal palace on the other side.

What Ezekiel foresees, in modern terms, is a strong government and a strong Church, each free from domination by the other, each deeply concerned with the health and strength of the other. He sees the State as a divinely appointed agency, and the Church as a divinely appointed agency. The two are separate, but partners.

Voltaire proclaimed that the world will be a blessed place when the neck of the last politician is strangled with the guts of the last priest. Karl Marx and his followers enthusiastically adopted the idea. They tried to do away with religious institutions, and promised that the State would, in time, wither away likewise. As one looks at the Communist countries, one gathers that the State is not withering very fast. While people are living together, there must be some form of government (though I believe we could survive with a great deal less than we have). And while there are people we likewise need the Church, the visible Body of Christ on earth, whose members consider themselves in fact the Savior's hands and feet.

I do not know what form the Church will take tomorrow. I suspect, indeed I pray, that it may differ greatly from that today. I hope that our children will be more successful than their fathers have been in resolving the tension between freedom and order. I hope they will be able to express the timeless faith in their own idiom — both the spoken and the sung word — better than we have. I hope they will leave in the disgraceful past the bickering that is so commonplace today. I hope they will place far more attention upon the gospel than the visible institution, in direct opposition to our practice. I anticipate many things about the Church tomorrow, but not its disappearance.

If we may judge from recorded history, people tomorrow will be in many ways like people today: born with immeasurable possibilities for glory or for shame. They will continue to need the Way and the Truth and the Life. They will continue to need private worship. They will continue to need public worship. As long as there are people here on earth, they will need the Church. Until the gates of hell finally are battered in, the Church will be here.

DATE DUE

MAR 3 1 '78			
MAY 3 1 '83			

DEMCO 38-297